· THAI ·
COOKING

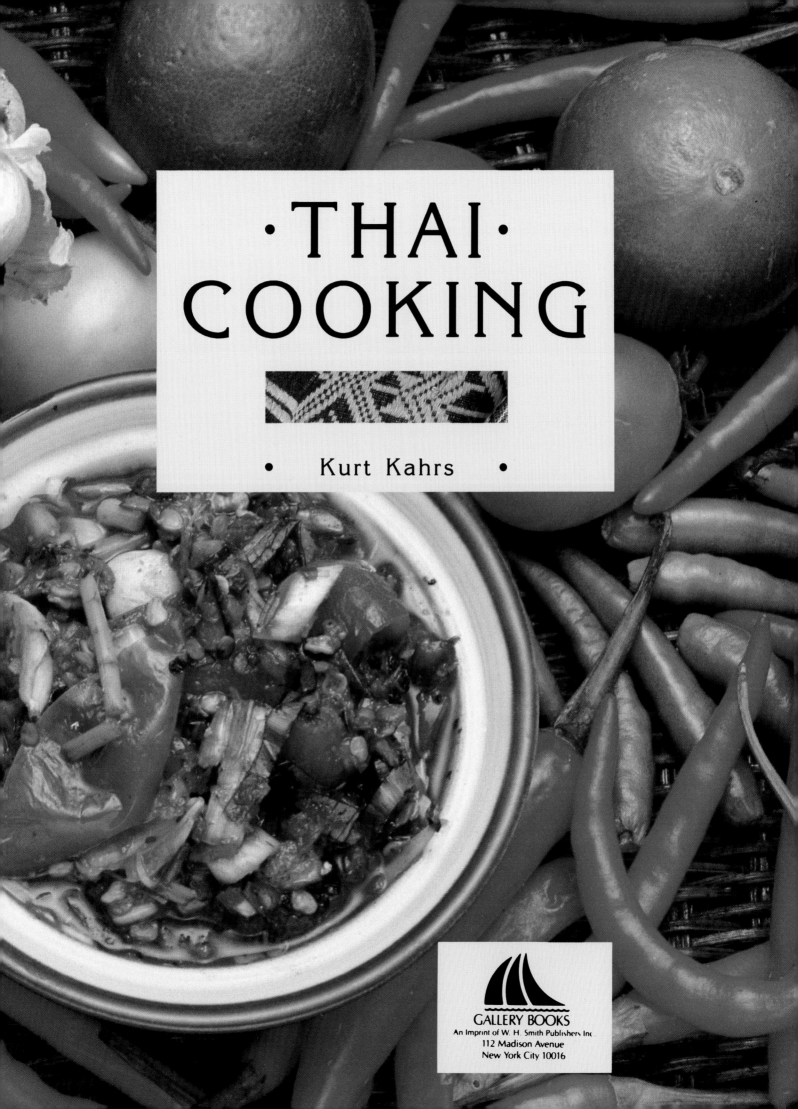

·THAI· COOKING

· Kurt Kahrs ·

GALLERY BOOKS
An Imprint of W. H. Smith Publishers Inc.
112 Madison Avenue
New York City 10016

A QUINTET BOOK
produced for
GALLERY BOOKS
An imprint of W.H. Smith Publishers Inc.
112 Madison Avenue
New York, New York 10016

ISBN 0-8317-87244

The book was designed and produced by
Quintet Publishing Limited
6 Blundell Street
London N7 9BH

Creative Director: Peter Bridgewater
Art Director: Ian Hunt
Designer: Annie Moss
Project Editor: Caroline Beattie
Contributing Editor: Joanna Lorenz
Photographer: Neyla Freeman

Typeset in Great Britain by
Central Southern Typesetters, Eastbourne
Manufactured in Hong Kong by Regent
Publishing Services Limited
Printed in Hong Kong by
Kwong Fat Offset Printing Company Limited

ACKNOWLEDGEMENTS

*My sincere thanks go to Miss Saing Poukwan, who coordinated the cooking
and without whose assistance this book would not have been possible. Also, to
Ancharee Premruthai, Ratchada Chisang, Nittaya Praratkun and Nujaree
Ruason for their help in the kitchen, and Jurirat Rongpaopong for her help
with the arrangements. Thanks also to Siriporn Buranaphan for the kind loan
of many of the props, and to Mr Virasoot Kunanugon, owner of Suktawee
Appartments, for the use of his facilities.*

DEDICATION

*I would like to thank my brother Danny for inducing (coercing) me into
coming to Thailand, and for all his help since. My thanks also to my sister for
introducing me to the sweeter side of cooking, and to my parents for helping
me start my career as a chef and for showing me that good food, like life, is to
be enjoyed.*

CONTENTS

INTRODUCTION

No other national cuisine has enjoyed the surge in popularity that Thai food has. A decade or so ago it was a rarity in Europe and most of the United States, and before that virtually unknown. In just a few years Thai cooking has emerged from relative obscurity to become one of the West's favourite exotic styles of cooking.

Even more important than the proliferation of restaurants is the growing availability of the ingredients that make this South-east Asian cuisine so distinctive. Little by little – at least in the major cities – Thai delicatessens and supermarkets are opening, and the better ones now sell fresh Thai vegetables and fruits. For more and more Western cooks it is becoming quite practical to attempt authentic versions of the majority of Thai dishes. There is a kind of snowball effect at work here: as people become more familiar with the popular recipes, the demand for the ingredients increases, and it becomes more worthwhile for the shops to import them. Competition among Thai foodstuff manufacturers means that there is ultimately a better choice on the shelves in the West. In just the last two or three years I've noticed the better brands of curry pastes that I buy here in Bangkok reach stores in New York and London.

The framework for this rich and varied cuisine is the basic culinary tradition of South-east Asia: rice- and noodle-based, more fish and vegetables than meat, more light meat than dark, and above all, spices and chillies for flavouring. It is this last element – the central role of spices – that is for most people the immediate characteristic of Thai food; indeed, what helps to raise Thai cooking to the status of a major cuisine is its inspired and eclectic use of spices.

Probably the second thing that makes Thai cooking challenging and interesting is the sheer variety of types of dish. Both of these distinctive qualities – spices and variety – stem from the same fundamental cause, the country's position at the crossroads of South-east Asia. Thailand lies between two Asian cuisines, Chinese and Indian, and has drawn extensively on both. Of course, Thailand is more than just a crossroads for food; peoples, culture, politics, art, every aspect of life is reflected in what has become an essentially Thai ability to absorb outside influences and blend them into something that is unique. Its position in straddling both mainland and maritime South-east Asia has meant that Siam, as it was known until well into this century, has never had the choice of being isolated. In order to survive, the country has taken waves of influence over the centuries from its neighbours.

Nevertheless, simply placing Thai cooking on the culinary map somewhere between China and India is an over-simplification. Most of the influence has not been direct, but by proxy, through its neighbouring countries. These include Burma, Laos, Cambodia and Malaysia, and each has had an effect on Thailand at different stages of its history. What the Thais have shown is a remarkable talent for taking the best of each and combining them in a highly distinctive way.

Some of the ingredients, and therefore some of the characteristics of the dishes, come from even further away. Chillies, which might seem after the first few meals to be quintessentially Thai, are originally from Central and South America. (Ordinary pepper, interestingly, goes under the name *phrik thai* – literally, 'Thai chilli', and pre-dates the fiery green and red chillies that Portuguese traders brought from the New World via Europe in the 16th century; even this, though, came at some earlier stage from the Moluccas of the East Indies.) Thai food must certainly have been different without chillies, but the enthusiasm with which they have been incorporated into so many dishes of the national diet is undeniable. Certainly, Thai cooks lost no time making up for the relatively late arrival of chillies.

Taken all together, these influences from abroad, such as Indian flavours via Burma, Muslim dishes from Malaysia, sticky rice and rustic, bitter flavours from Laos, and stir-fried wok cooking and steamed fish dishes from the Chinese immigrant population, have made Thai cooking a strongly regional set of cuisines. In a typical Thai restaurant in the West this is not immediately obvious, and many of the more interesting dishes are excluded from the menu for being too 'provincial'. (Also, the predominance of Thai-Chinese ownership of restaurants means that, naturally, there are more Chinese-style dishes offered.) Here in Thailand, however, a typical meal served in the Northeast, on the banks of the Mekong River facing across to Laos, is quite different from one served in the Muslim South, close to the Malaysian border.

OPPOSITE PAGE *Cooking in a wok. This food seller ferries up and down the market all day.* **LEFT** *Itinerant food vendors are found throughout Thailand, selling sweets or savouries.* **RIGHT** *The famous floating market, Khun Pitak, near Bangkok.*

This regional variety is what has appealed to me more and more since I have lived here in Bangkok. Travelling whenever I have been able, I have collected the distinctive recipes from each of Thailand's regions. The most distinctive are undoubtedly the South, North and North-east, mainly because in a culinary way they have remained isolated the longest – it has never been easy, until the last couple of years, to find Bangkok restaurants with extensive dishes from these parts of the country. Nevertheless, the Gulf of Thailand, the Central Plains and Bangkok itself are also significant culinary regions. The Gulf, of course, has supplied the country with the majority of its seafood dishes; the Central Plains, where most of Thailand's rice is grown, is the heartland for traditional Thai cooking; Bangkok, as well as being the country's cultural melting plot, is also distinctive for the cuisine of its ethnic Chinese population and for Royal, or Palace, cooking.

THE THAI KITCHEN

A traditional Thai kitchen reflects, in its layout and its contents, both the living conditions of this tropical country and its basic cooking styles. It is built around the stove, which can vary from a built-in range of tiled cement to a simple earthenware charcoal pot. All cooking is done over open heat sources, never enclosed, so an oven is unnecessary. As there is a large amount of frying over high heat involved, ventilation is an important concern, and in many old-style houses the kitchen is actually a separate building, with slatted walls.

Of course, traditional kitchen design, like many traditional Thai ways of life, are changing extremely rapidly. Thailand for many years now has been enjoying an economic boom; as Thais replace the older wooden houses with concrete structures and European designs (apartment blocks particularly, in Bangkok), their kitchens come more and more to resemble Western ones.

Nevertheless, some of the original principles persist. Steaming, boiling and frying are the main cooking techniques, so it is the hob of a cooker that is used, not the oven. One of the essentially Chinese traditions that has been adopted by the Thais is a considerable amount of rapid cooking over a high heat – stir-fried dishes in a *kata* (wok) are prominent in the cuisine. This means it is a considerable advantage to have a strong source of open heat. Charcoal cooking is, naturally, out of the question in the West, but gas is more useful than electricity.

The year-round hot climate has also had an effect on Thai cooking and the kitchen. Until recently, neither refrigerators nor air-conditioning were widely available, and Thai cooking evolved to cope with conditions in which food does not keep for long. Traditionally, most food is bought daily at the market, and there are few dishes constructed from leftovers (rice dishes are an exception: *khao phad,* or fried rice, is the basic Thai leftover recipe). In addition, there is a large range of preserved foodstuffs: pickled, sun-dried, salted and fermented. A selection of some of the most well-known includes pickled garlic *(krathiam dong)*, dried chillies and dried fish *(phrik haeng* and *plaa haeng)*, salted eggs *(khai khem)* and fish sauce *(nam plaa)*. These, and perhaps some pre-cooked rice, are traditionally stored in a larder cupboard protected from flies by mesh screens, and from ants by putting the cupboard legs in bowls of water. Nowadays, however, the refrigerator is taking over.

COOKING TECHNIQUES AND EQUIPMENT

The basic cooking utensils are the *kata* (wok), saucepan and steamer. Because maximum heat transmission is important in wok cooking a flat-bottomed wok is generally more useful. In stir-frying, the important technique is to add just a little oil but to bring this to a very high heat very quickly (to minimize burning and smoke). The food to be stir-fried is added all at once and moved around constantly with a spatula, while rocking the wok at the same time. The point about the high heat is to seal in the juices and flavour of the individual pieces so that they stay crisp and tasty. Slow stir-frying produces limp, partially steamed vegetables. A tip for dealing with hard, solid vegetables is not only to cut them into small pieces but, after a minute or two of stir-frying, to turn off the heat (or turn it right down) and cover the wok with a large saucepan lid. This has the effect of adding a little steaming.

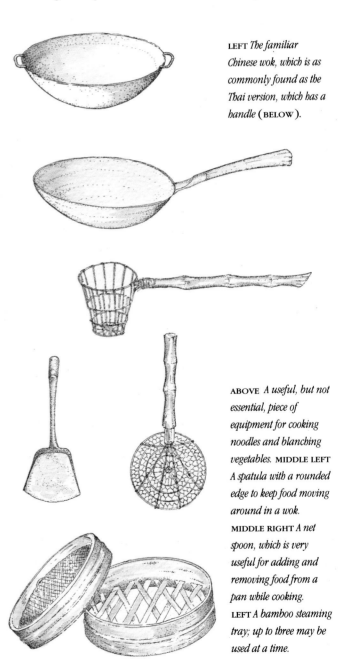

LEFT *The familiar Chinese wok, which is as commonly found as the Thai version, which has a handle (*BELOW*).*

ABOVE *A useful, but not essential, piece of equipment for cooking noodles and blanching vegetables.* MIDDLE LEFT *A spatula with a rounded edge to keep food moving around in a wok.* MIDDLE RIGHT *A net spoon, which is very useful for adding and removing food from a pan while cooking.* LEFT *A bamboo steaming tray; up to three may be used at a time.*

For boiled dishes, such as *kwitiaow nam* and *khao tom kai*, a deep saucepan is necessary. For adding and removing ingredients, Thais use attractively made bamboo-handled brass wire mesh baskets and scoops, but a large perforated or slotted spoon or sieve will do as well. A saucepan is also needed for cooking plain rice, but nowadays in Thailand any family that can afford one will have an electric rice-steamer. The results are more reliable for an inexperienced cook, and save time.

Steaming is the third main technique, used for many fish dishes, for example, *haw mok plaa*. The standard utensil for this in Thailand is an aluminium Chinese steamer set, consisting of a saucepan for the water, on top of which fits one or more perforated trays, and a lid for the top. These are not expensive, and are available in Chinese supermarkets, but a makeshift alternative is a colander suspended over a deep saucepan, again with a lid large enough to seal in the steam. Do not overfill the saucepan base with water, but make sure it does not dry out during the steaming process. One traditional Thai steaming method is to wrap food in parcels of leaves: this imparts some of the leaf's flavour to the food, and looks very attractive when served. Banana leaves are the standard, but pandanus leaves *(bai toei)* also make a good wrapping.

One of the most important features of Thai cooking is the emphasis on preparation. Very many of the recipes here are actually cooked quite quickly, and with a minimum of complication, but much more time is taken up with preparing the ingredients. Often this is mainly a matter of peeling, chopping, and arranging into piles: with wok-cooked dishes you will usually need to add ingredients in rapid succession, so they should be close to the cooker and easy to scoop up. If you are entertaining guests to a Thai dinner, you may find that some of the dishes have to be cooked at the very last moment, so arrange your pre-dinner drinks accordingly! This is an additional reason for varying the types of cooked dish in a menu: steamed dishes can be left to cook by themselves, but fried dishes need constant last-minute attention.

Basic equipment for preparation includes a chopping board (better still, two), a cleaver or large kitchen knife, medium and small kitchen knives, and a mortar and pestle. Professional Thai cooks use a Chinese cleaver for virtually all cutting jobs, and handle them with considerable delicacy, but if you are used to Western-style knives, use one of those. It must, however, be kept perfectly sharp.

There are two kinds of mortar and pestle used in Thailand. One, for lighter work, is a relatively deep, rough ceramic mortar and wooden pestle; the pounding action is up and down. The second kind is for heavy-duty pounding; both the mortar and pestle are made from heavy stone, like granite, and the cross-section of the inside of the mortar is shallower and more or less circular. Pounding with these involves a grinding action as well. A blender or food processor can also be used for pounding larger quantities of ingredients.

Decorative fruit and vegetable carving

The carving of fruit and vegetables occupies a special place in Thai Royal or Palace-style cooking. This decorative preparation of raw ingredients is a study in itself, but at a simpler level it provides an attractive touch to a Thai meal (for instance) if you carve rather than just chop vegetables for dips, such as *nam phrik ong*. The essential equipment is not complicated: a sharp paring knife with a finely pointed blade and a bowl of water, preferably iced, to prevent discoloration of the carved pieces. It is definitely time-consuming, although how much so depends on the degree of elaboration you go for.

One of the simplest cuts for smallish round vegetables such as tomatoes and *makheua puang* (pea aubergine) is to halve them by means of consecutive diagonal cuts. Chillies can be given a flower-like appearance by making two deep cuts through the length of the chilli, at right angles to each other, from the tip to near the base. Hold the stem on the chopping board so that the chilli lies flat and cut straight down and through from the tip end. Scrape out the seeds and drop the chilli into a bowl of iced water; the ends will curve outwards naturally. You can create a similar effect with a spring onion (scallion): first cut it

down to the point where the stem begins to turn from white to green, hold this end with one hand, and then make the same kind of deep lengthwise cuts from the bulb end. As with the chillies, these white ends will curve outwards; store temporarily in the bowl of cold water.

Cucumbers are an easy vegetable to carve designs onto, for not only are they firm, but the contrast between the dark skin and the pale flesh underneath makes surface designs very effective – rather like making a cameo. Cut the design just through the skin. Another common Thai treatment for cucumbers is to carve them into leaf shapes. Thai cucumbers are smaller and so lend themselves to this, but with the larger European and American cucumbers, you will need to cut thick slices down to a basic leaf shape.

PLANNING A THAI MENU

To fit in with normal Western eating habits, most foreigners are likely to try one, or perhaps two, Thai dishes when cooking at home. The European and American dinner menu is usually starter, main course, and dessert. Thai food can work perfectly well in this way; you could begin, for instance, with a spicy soup like *tom yum kung*, continue with, say, a beef curry like *panaeng neua*, and finish with the popular baked custard dessert *sangkhyaa*.

In Thailand, however, people eat rather differently, and you will get the best out of this marvellously varied cuisine by following a more authentic Thai menu style. To begin with, eating in Thailand is rarely a solitary affair. Thais prefer to eat in company, and a large group of people is better than a few. One good reason for this is that then the entire table can share in a great variety of dishes, and sharing is an important part of Thai etiquette.

At a Thai dinner table, guests have individual plates, a fork and spoon, and if there is a soup it is usual for each person to have a small bowl as well, normally with a ceramic Chinese spoon. The food – several dishes, which may arrive all together or at different times during the meal – is placed in the centre of the table, and guests help themselves (or, more politely, serve their neighbours). Rice is central to the meal, and is either placed in a large bowl on the table or served by the host to each guest. The order of eating is unimportant: typically, people start with a small helping from one dish, add it to the rice, then move on to another dish, using the same plate and the same mound of rice. On the whole, however, dishes are not mixed on the plate.

As the range of recipes in this book shows, the great majority of Thai dishes are chopped, mixed and stirred in such a way that the largest piece is usually bite-sized. Only a very few dishes, such as stuffed chicken wings or large river prawns, are irreducable and must be taken as individual portions. This, of course, makes it a lot easier to cater for surprise guests: the quantities are simply increased, or an extra dish added.

Ideally, there should be a balance of the type of dish served. There are no strict rules, it is simply a matter of commonsense. For instance, a well-balanced dinner for six people might have, in addition to the rice, a curry, a salad, a soup, a small *nam phrik* (chilli sauce dip), a fried dish and a steamed fish. These would all be served more or less together (soup accompanies the meal and does not, as in the West, precede the main dishes), or the steamed fish might be served slightly

later. After the main meal, you would serve fruit and possibly a cooked dessert. In addition, you might also decide to serve a few snacks, such as *kratong thong,* with drinks before sitting down to the table.

As for quantities, the servings given for each recipe are a guide, but it will depend on the number of dishes you intend to serve at one dinner, your appetite, and also how chilli-hot you prepare the food. The more chillies in a dish, the smaller amounts everyone will take (but the more rice).

THAI FOOD NAMES

The Thai language, like the cuisine, has evolved from a mixture of sources, ultimately Chinese and Indian. The spoken language is a member of the Tai group, which encompasses Southern China, Laos, the Shan States of Burma, and Assam. The Chinese influence is most immediately obvious in the high proportion of single-syllable words and in the tones.

It is the tones that give most Westerners the greatest trouble in pronouncing Thai correctly, as the meaning of many words changes completely with the pitch of the voice. There are five tones in Thai: middle, high, low, and the two most difficult for untrained ears, rising and falling. The Thais have a number of deliberate tongue-twisters that highlight the importance of tones, such as 'mai mai mai mai', meaning, with the appropriate rise and fall in pitch, 'green wood doesn't burn', a sort of Thai 'Peter Piper picked a peck of pickled peppers'!

The written Thai language, however, makes it quite clear to the initiated how the words should be pronounced, and the attractive script that you can see on supermarket packets of imported Thai spices and the like shows the Indian influence on the language. It comes from the Devanagari system of writing that spread from India via Cambodia. By and large, as in our own Roman alphabet, each symbol represents a letter, and words are written left to right (although vowels can be above, below, before or after consonants, or even not written at all!).

Although there is an official system of transliterating Thai into the Roman alphabet, it is not as useful as it could be. It ignores, for instance, the fact that some letters are pronounced quite differently when they appear at the end of a word (the Thai word for sugar literally reads 'nam taal' but is pronounced 'nam taan'). In any case, as far as menus are concerned, there are almost as many systems as there are restaurants, and many Thai restaurateurs simply follow their whims.

In this book, I've adapted the Haas phonetic system, with the following conventions:

Consonants

The glottal stop, quite common in spoken Thai. Make it sound like the end of the Cockney version of 'what' – that is, with the last letter virtually dropped off.

kh, ph, th These are aspirated versions of k, p. and t; as in the English 'key', 'pin', and 'ten', but pronounced in a breathy way. Ph, as in the name of the resort island of Phuket, does not sound like f!

ng   As in the English 'sing'; the g is not pronounced separately.

r   Pronounced distinctly, as in the English 'red'. In Bangkok in particular, many Thais interchange r and l.

All other consonants are as you would expect.

Vowels

a	As in 'sad'
aa	Long version of a, as in 'father'
e	As in 'red'
ae	As in 'air', with the r unpronounced
oe	As in 'her', with the r unpronounced
o	As in 'song'
aw	As in 'law'
o	As in 'tone'
i	As in 'pin'
ii	As in 'peek'
ia	As in the name 'Ian'
u	As in 'wood'
oo	As in 'soon'
ai	As in 'mine'
eu	A difficult one. Raise the centre of the tongue and keep the lips relaxed but wide.
eu	The long version of eu above. Equally difficult.
ao	As in 'cloud'

ahaan: food
ba mii: egg noodles
bai: leaf
bai horapa: sweet basil
bai karii: curry leaf
bai kluai: banana leaf
bai krapao: holy basil
bai krawaan: bay leaf
bai makrut: kaffir lime leaf
bai mangluk: lemon basil
bai saranae: mint
bai toei: pandanus leaf
chaam: bowl
chawn: spoon
champoo: rose apple
dawkjan: mace
dip: raw
dok kluai: banana flower
dong: pickled
fak: bitter gourd (bitter melon)
farang: foreign
haeng: dried
hawm lek: shallot
hed hom: dried mushroom
hed hoonoo: wood fungus/mouse-ear mushroom
hoi: shellfish, shell
hoi malaeng poo: mussel
hoi naang rom: oyster
hoi shell: scallop
huad: steamer for sticky rice
huajai: heart
jaan: plate
ka: galangal/laos

kaan ploo: cloves
kaeng: curry
kaeng cheud: clear soup
kaeo: glass
kai: chicken
kalamplii: cabbage
kamin: turmeric
kanoon: jackfruit
kapi: shrimp paste
karii: Indian-style curry
kata: wok
keun chai: celery
khai: egg
khai khem: salted egg
khanom chiin: nest of rice noodles
khao: rice
khao hom malii: jasmine-scented rice
khao niaow: sticky/glutinous rice
khao phad: fried rice
khao plao: steamed rice
khao suay: cooked rice
khem: salty
khiao: green
khing: ginger
khom: bitter
khrog: mortar
khuad: bottle
kluai: banana
kob: frog
krachai: rhizome, lesser galangal, ginger root

krajab: water-chestnut
kratai: rabbit
krathiam: garlic
khrathiam dong: pickled garlic
kreung kaeng: curry base
kreung nai: entrails
kung foi: prawns
kung haeng: dried shrimp
kung narng: shrimp
kwitiaow: rice noodles
laab: spicy minced (ground) meat
lamut: sapodilla
lamyai: longan
laos: galangal/ka
lin: tongue
linchii: lichee
lon: cooked sauce
look chiin: fish ball
look chiin neua: meat ball
lookjan: nutmeg
ma muang: mango
mafeung: star apple
makhaam: tamarind
makheua puang: pea aubergine (eggplant)
makheua thaed: tomato
makneua khun: round aubergine (eggplant)
makheua yao: aubergine (egg-plant)
makrut: kaffir lime
malakaw: papaya
malii: jasmine
mann: yam
man farang: potato
man samrong: tapioca
manao: lime
maphrao: coconut
met: seed, nut
met ma muang: cashew nut
mii: noodles
miid: knife
mongkut: mangosteen
moo: pork
mussaman: Muslim
nam: water
nam kathii: coconut milk
nam man: oil
nam man hoi: oyster sauce
nam manao: lime juice
nam phrik: chilli sauce (many varieties)
nam plaa: fermented fish sauce

nam siew: Chinese soya sauce
nam som: orange juice, vinegar
nam som makhaam: tamarind water
nam taan: sugar
nam taan peuk: palm sugar
neua: beef
ngaa: sesame
ngaw: rambutan
noi naa: custard apple
nok: bird
nok krachab: small rice-bird
nok krathaa: quail
normai: bamboo shoot
ob cheuy: cinnamon
op: bake
ped: duck
paeng: flour
pew makrut: kaffir lime zest
phad: stir-fried
phak: vegetable (particularly greens)
phak bung: morning glory (swamp cabbage)
phakchii: coriander
phakchii farang: parsley
phao: roast
phed: chilli-hot
phonlamai: fruit
phriaw: sour
phrik: chilli pepper
phrik chiifaa: finger-sized chillies
phrik haeng: dried chillies
phirk kii noo: small, very hot chillies
phrik num: Northern, medium-sized green chillies
phrik thai: black pepper
phrik thai sod: green pepper-corns
phrik yawk: sweet bell pepper
piik: wing
ping: roasted, baked, barbecued
plaa: fish
plaa haeng: dried fish
plaa khem: salted fish
plaa meuk: squid
plaa raa: thick, fermented fish sauce
poi kak bua: star anise
poo: crab
puak: taro
raadnaa: topped with

raan ahaan: restaurant
rawn: hot
saa kwitiaow: wire-mesh noodle basket
saag: pestle
sai: intestines
sangkhyaa: baked custard
sapparod: pineapple
sataw: Thai flat beans
sawm: fork
sen lek: thin rice noodles
sen mii: rice vermicelli noodles
sen yai: wide, flat rice noodles
sod: fresh
som: orange
som aw: pomelo
somsaa: citron
sors phrik: chilli sauce
taeng kwa: cucumber
tai: south
takiab: chopsticks
takrai: lemon grass
talaad: market

taohoo: bean curd (tofu)
taohooyii: pickled bean curd (tofu)
tao jiaw: salted soya beans
tap: liver
thalae: sea
thong: gold
thua: bean
thua ngawk: bean sprouts
thurian: durian
tod: fried (individual pieces)
ton hom: spring onion (scallion)
toon: steamed
waan: sweet
woon sen: cellophane or glass noodles
yad sai: stuffed
yam: salad
yang: roast
yen: cold
yiiraa: cumin
yod: top, tip

INGREDIENTS

AUBERGINE/EGGPLANT *(makheua yao)* There are a number of different varieties of aubergine in Thailand, none of them quite the same as Western aubergines. They range in shape from small and round to long and thin, and in colour from purple to yellow, white and striped. The *makheua yao* variety (literally 'long aubergine') most closely resembles those on sale in Europe and America. Another kind of aubergine, round and hard, is *makheua khun,* which has a crunchy texture but little flavour: it is used as a raw vegetable accompaniment to *laab* (spicy minced/ground meat) and in some curries. See also pea aubergine/ eggplant.

BASIL *(bai horapa, bai mangluk, bai krapao)* These three varieties are each slightly different, which really matters only when more than one is being used as a vegetable garnish to a meat salad. *Bai horapa,* sweet basil, is the most common, and resembles the European and American basil. *Bai mangluk* is also sometimes known as lemon basil. *Bai krapao,* or holy basil, is more unusual, with reddish-purple leaves.

BAMBOO SHOOT *(normai)* A long, fibrous shoot with a white central core. Usually bought canned, ready-peeled and par-boiled.

BANANA *(kluai)* The Western experience with bananas is normally limited to the large, rather hard and mildly flavoured fruit imported from Central America. Thai cooks, on the other hand, have a choice of

LEFT *A busy covered market in Bangkok. Traditionally, food shopping is done every day, extremely early in the morning.*

RIGHT *A selection of dried fish, shrimps and squids.*

more than two dozen varieties. The most commonly used are dwarf bananas, much smaller and sweeter than those normally available in a Western supermarket. Unripe, green bananas are also used.

BANANA LEAVES (*bai kluai*) Are used for wrapping and cooking food in; dark green, inedible and huge, they are often cut into smaller pieces for use. Banana flowers (*dok kluai*) are also used – the heart of the flower is sliced and eaten.

BEAN CURD/TOFU (*taohoo*) This white curd, normally about the consistency of a caramel custard, is made from unfermented soya bean paste. It is available in 'firm' and 'soft' forms.

BEAN SPROUTS (*thua ngawk*) Sprouted mung beans, eaten raw or steamed, and used in stir-fries, soups and salads.

CELERY (*keun chai*) A more delicate and smaller vegetable than the Western variety. As a substitute, use only the small young leaves from the centre of a Western celery stalk.

CHILLIES/CHILIES (*phrik*) Chillies are so characteristic of modern Thai cooking that it seems strange to many people that they were originally an import from the New World. They arrived with Portuguese traders, probably in the sixteenth century, and the enthusiasm with which they have been incorporated into Thai cuisine shows that they obviously fulfilled a latent need for strong, fiery flavour.

The Thais use a variety of chillies, although not as extensive as the range available in Latin America, with different degrees of fieriness. The colour is green when immature, changing to yellow, orange and red as they ripen. The smallest and hottest are *phrik kii noo*, which translates with characteristic Thai lack of euphemism as 'mouse dropping chillies' (apart from the colour, there is some similarity of shape!). Other chillies are *phrik chiifaa*, which are finger-sized, and *phrik num*, which are a Northern variety, and slightly larger. (The larger, mild capsicums are called *phrik yawk*, our sweet or bell peppers.)

Chillies can be stored for up to about a week in a sealed, dry container in a refrigerator; after that they begin to grow mould and blacken. Chillies are also sun-dried, in which form they can be stored indefinitely. These appear wrinkled and crisp, with a colour from deep red to brown-black.

The hottest part of a chilli are the seeds, and if you wish you can remove these by holding the steam in one hand and slicing down the length of the chilli with the tip of a sharp knife, scraping out the seeds and interior ribs with the knife tip. Dried chillies can be seeded simply

by breaking off the stem, holding the open end of the chilli so that it is pointing down, and rolling it between your fingers; the seeds just fall out. Note, however, that Thais normally leave the seeds in; the fieriness is, after all, the main point of using chillies. Needles to say, be careful of the oil when handling chillies; never rub your eyes, for example, before washing your hands thoroughly.

Chillies can be used whole, sliced or pounded. You can also buy them in flakes and ground as chilli powder and cayenne pepper.

CHILLI SAUCE (*sors phrik*) A condiment or paste made from chillies, salt, sugar and vinegar, available in bottles in various strengths.

COCONUTS AND COCONUT MILK (*maphrao* and *nam kathii*) As in virtually every other country where the coconut tree forms a natural part of the landscape, it plays an important part in the traditional economy. The whole tree, from fruit to palm fronds, is made use of. In Thai cooking, its contribution is mainly for the milk, used as a thickening and flavouring for various curries and meat, vegetable and fish dishes, as well as in sweets, desserts and drinks.

It is important to distinguish between two kinds of coconut milk: 'thick' and 'thin'. Both are made from the shredded meat of mature coconuts, and have nothing to do with the refreshing water content of the young green fruit. The dry coconut is cracked open and the white meat scraped out; the meat is then shredded, placed in boiling water, and squeezed to express the milky liquid. This first pressing produces 'thick' coconut milk; repeated squeezings with fresh water produce the 'thin' milk. The problem in the West is obtaining ripe coconuts; the closest substitute is grated unsweetened, or desiccated, coconut. You may find better results by using cow's milk instead of water, or a mixture of milk and water. This is the authentic method of preparation, but an acceptable substitute is canned coconut milk. Blocks of creamed coconut can also be used; just stir into warm water.

To make coconut milk in this way, use 2½ cups/20 fl oz/550 ml of grated dried coconut and 4 cups/32 fl oz/900 ml of liquid (water, water-and-milk or milk) to make 2½ cups/20 fl oz/550 ml of 'thick' coconut milk. Bring the water to the boil in a saucepan or, if you are using milk, scald it. Add the coconut, stir, remove from the heat and allow to cool. Strain and press through a sieve until the residue is dry. Add more water or milk if you want to make a second pressing for 'thin' coconut milk. You can refrigerate it for several days.

CORIANDER/CILANTRO/Chinese parsley (*phakchii*) Coriander is as easy to grow as parsley, which it resembles. It adds a distinctive flavour that is very characteristic of Thai and also Cambodian food. The fresh leaves are commonly used as a garnish, but for cooking the roots and stems are also used. In the West, the stems are usually sold trimmed without the root, but they can be cut off and frozen when you are lucky enough to find them with roots. Coriander seeds (*met phakchii*) are also used dried as a spice, whole and ground.

CUCUMBER (*taeng kwa*) Thai cucumbers are smaller and shorter than the Western variety, but this makes little difference in use, which is as a raw vegetable accompaniment to such dishes as *laab* (spicy minced/ground meat), and chopped in dishes such as *ajaad*, a salad.

DRIED FISH (*plaa haeng*) Salty and pungent, these sun- or smoke-dried fish are a staple of Thai cuisine but less commonly available in the West. The very small herring-like dried fish, about an inch (2.5 cm) long, make a tasty snack when deep-fried for a few seconds. Dried

LEFT *Threshing rice by machine near Ayutthaya.*

shrimps *(kung haeng),* whole, ground and as paste, are a common Thai seasoning.

DRIED MUSHROOMS *(hed hom)* Available from Chinese supermarkets, these add a distinctly Chinese flavour to dishes such as clear soups. Soak them in warm water until soft before use. See also wood fungus.

FISH SAUCE *(nam plaa)* An essential ingredient in Thai cooking and as a condiment. Salty and fermented, it is highly distinctive, a clear brown liquid sold in bottles. Use either the Thai version, *nam plaa,* or the Vietnamese *nuoc mam;* they are virtually identical. In cooking, use straight from the bottle; for using as a condiment, serve in small Chinese sauce dishes with 2 or 3 chopped small chillies *(phrik kii noo)* and a squeeze of lime juice. Fish sauce is rich in salt and some nitrogen; guests sprinkle a few drops, taken with a spoon, on dishes in much the same way that salt and pepper are used at a Western table.

GALANGAL *(ka or laos)* A ginger-like rhizome, similar in appearance but milder in flavour. Sometimes also known as Siamese ginger. It is used in a similar way as ginger: fresh, dried and ground.

GARLIC *(krathiam)* This is used extensively in Thai cooking, pounded with a mortar and pestle, sometimes added whole, or sliced and deep-fried to make golden flakes. Thai garlic cloves are rather different from those in Europe and America, not only considerably smaller, but with a skin thin enough to be used in cooking. In the recipies, it is assumed that the larger Western cloves are used, and peeled. Garlic is also available pickled and marinated in vinegar *(krathiam dong).*

GINGER *(khing)* The fresh ginger normally available in the West is a little drier and harder than the young, pale pink or yellow roots available in Thailand in the rainy season. As well as an ingredient, raw slices accompany Issaan dishes such as *sai krok issaan.* Used fresh, peeled and sliced or pounded, or dried and ground. Ginger is also available candied. See also galangal and *krachai.*

KAFFIR LIME *(makrut)* One of the most distinctive flavours of Thailand, this is a knobbly dark green fruit, of which only the aromatic zest *(pew makrut)* and leaves *(bai makrut)* are used in cooking – the juice makes a traditional hair shampoo. Use lime zest and citrus leaves as substitutes if you can't find the real thing, with dried kaffir lime to supplement the flavour.

KRACHAI There is no generally accepted English word for this small, yellow-brown rhizome related to ginger and galangal *(ka or laos),* although it is sometimes called lesser galangal, finger root or rhizome. An ingredient used, when available, in fish curries.

LEMON GRASS *(takrai)* This gives a lemony flavour to dishes, but is more aromatic than the lemon fruit. The lower several inches of the stalk are used, from the whitish 'bulb'. In soups and curries, the fibrous stalks are usually partly crushed by pounding with the back of a knife and removed before serving; another use is in some salads, in which case the stalks are cut into thin rings (it may be necessary to peel off the outer, more fibrous leaves). Available fresh, dried and ground.

LIME *(manao)* The juice is used in cooking and drinks, and the zest can be used as a substitute for that of the kaffir lime. Thai limes are smaller, darker and sweeter than those commonly available in the West.

MANGO *(ma muang)* There are a number of varieties of mango, varying in shape, size and colour. The best Thai variety is *okrong.* Thai mangoes have yellow skins, and while the ripe fruit is sweet, it lacks the heavy aromatic flavour of Indian *alfonsos.* As a dessert, mangoes are eaten ripe, but small slices of the tart green mango are used in salads and also eaten as a snack with salt and sugar. Mangoes are also available canned and dried.

NOODLES *(mii)* There are many types of noodle eaten in Thailand, the most common being rice noodles *(kwitiaow),* cellophane or glass noodles *(woon sen)* and egg noodles *(ba mii).*

Rice noodles are available in three sizes: wide and flat (*sen yai*, meaning 'big path'), spaghetti-sized (*sen lek*) and very thin vermicelli-sized (*sen mii*), also known as rice stick noodles. Sometimes sold fresh, they are usually dried and either deep-fried or soaked before using. Kwitiaow can also be bought in fresh, folded slabs, to be sliced to the width required.

Cellophane or glass noodles (also known as bean-thread or transparent noodles) are semi-clear and made from the dried, strained liquid of puréed mung beans; sold dried, they need to be soaked for 15 minutes before cooking.

Egg noodles are made from egg and wheat flour, and are sold fresh and dried, often in compressed parcels. They vary in size. Egg noodles are particularly popular in the Northern parts of Thailand close to Burma.

More information on cooking and serving noodles is given on page 17 ('The Central Plains').

PALM SUGAR (*nam taan peuk*) This thick, brown, almost wet sugar is made from the boiled sap of the Palmyra palm tree. It is usually available canned in the West.

PAPAYA/PAWPAW (*malakaw*) As with the mango, the papaya is eaten both ripe and unripe. Squeeze lime juice over ripe fruit before eating it. The unripe green fruit, shredded, is the basis of the famous North-eastern *som tam thai*. Thai papayas are larger than those normally available in the West.

PEA AUBERGINE/EGGPLANT (*makheua puang*) Looks rather like a large green pea, but has a distinctive fresh, bitter taste, and is used in some curries. Do not substitute with ordinary peas; the flavours are completely different, despite appearances.

PEPPERCORNS (*phrik thai*) Literally, 'Thai pepper', peppercorns were originally an import from the Moluccas. Black pepper was formerly used as a hot spice in Thai cooking before the introduction of chillies. White peppercorns are skinned fully riped versions. Both are used in cooking, whole, cracked and ground.

Green peppercorns (*phrik thai sod*) are the milder young, fresh version, rare but now becoming increasingly available in the West.

PINEAPPLE (*sapparod*) In cooking, the pineapple makes an appearance for its contrasting sweet flavour, as in *khaeug khua sapparod hoi malaeng poo*. It also forms the basis of the spectacular-looking *khao op sapparod*.

RICE (*khao*) Rice is the staple of Thai cooking, and while no Thai cook would give a second thought to preparing the day's rice, if you are not familiar with rice steaming techniques, it is important to perfect them. Thai rice is long-grain (Thai fragrant rice is world-renowned), and should be fluffy and well-separated when properly cooked. The easiest way by far is to use an electric rice cooker – a good investment if you eat rice regularly and a main item in modern Thai kitchens. Otherwise, use a saucepan in the following manner:

Wash the rice well with several changes of water until it runs clear. For 1 cup/8 oz/225 g of rice add 2½ cups/20 fl oz/550 ml of water; bring both together to the boil over a high heat. Turn the heat down to low, cover the pan and allow to cook for about 20 minutes. Fluff up the rice before serving. In Thai, cooked steamed rice is called *khao suay* or *khao plao*.

See also page 17 ('The Central Plains') and sticky rice.

SHRIMP PASTE (*kapi*) Traditionally, shrimp paste was a by-product of *nam plaa* (fish sauce), made from the pounded residue of shrimps and salt left to dry in the sun. Now, however, its manufacture is a Thai industry of its own. The best quality paste has a fine texture and is not very salty. The colour is either pinkish or dark brown; however, inferior quality *kapi* has colouring added to make it darker. It is available in the West in vacuum-sealed jars.

SOYA SAUCE (*nam siew*) This is an essential ingredient for most Chinese dishes, as a condiment at the table and for general cooking. Easily available, it is sold in two forms – white (light) and black (dark).

SPRING ONIONS/SCALLIONS (*ton hom*) Also known as salad onions, these elongated, mild members of the onion family are used sliced (both white and green parts) as a garnish for soups and salads.

STICKY OR GLUTINOUS RICE (*khao niaow*) Sometimes also called sweet rice. This is a different strain of rice from the familiar one, and forms an important part of the diet in the North-east of Thailand and parts of the North. The grains are short and opaque (rather than translucent in the case of ordinary rice). Use to accompany the regional dishes from these areas, and also for desserts such as *khao niaow ma muang*.

Sticky rice must be steamed, never boiled, and the secret of success is to soak it in cold water for a considerably time before cooking – up to several hours. This both cleans the grains and softens them, so that they do not clump together in glutinous masses.

In Issaan, the heartland of sticky rice, most cooks use a steaming basket woven from bamboo known as a *huad*. Filled with rice, this is fitted onto a wide-mouthed deep pan containing water. The ensemble is placed on the stove, and the steam from the boiling water cooks the rice in about 20 minutes (the time depends on how much soaking the rice has received). Turn the rice once during the steaming, as the lower part cooks more quickly. Well-cooked stick rice should be firm and dry, with the grains adhering to each other; neither hard, which is a sign of it having been cooked too long, nor gooey, which happens if you overcook it. A couscoussière, available in French kitchen supply shops, makes an ideal alternative; otherwise, line a large metal sieve or colander with muslin cloth, cover, and place over a large pan half full with boiling water.

SWEET BASIL, see basil.

TAMARIND (*makhaam*) This distinctive flavouring is obtained from the pulp of the pod of the tamarind tree. Tamarind liquid is used as a sour, bitter addition to many meat and fish dishes. Brown, sticky and sharp-tasting, the pulp can be bought fresh and moist (with or without the pod seeds and fibre, which should be removed) dried in blocks, or in concentrated form (which just needs diluting). If pulp is used, it needs soaking before use: the soaking liquid is then strained and squeezed out of the pulp.

TURMERIC (*kamin*) A spice, like cardamom and cloves, that features mainly in Indian and Muslim dishes. Sold as a fresh orange-coloured root (similar to ginger), it is more commonly available dried, whole and as an orange powder.

WOOD FUNGUS (*hed hoonoo*) A dried mushroom, also known as mouse-ear, cloud-ear or Chinese black fungus. Used in soups, stir-fries, chicken and fish dishes, the mushrooms must be soaked in several changes of warm water for 30 minutes or until they are soft before use; they have the consistency of jelly.

THE CENTRAL PLAINS

The heartland of the country is the broad valley and delta of the Chaophaya River and its tributaries. These flat, well-watered plains were the main route for the Tai settlers who populated the country from the North, and all of Thailand's successive capitals have been built here. When the Tais finally achieved independence from the Khmers in 1243, Sukhothai became the first capital, some 300 miles upriver. In 1350 the capital moved to Ayutthaya, closer to the sea, and finally, at the end of the 18th century, the present capital of Bangkok was founded in the delta. The fertile soil and abundant rainfall have made the Central Plains the kingdom's natural rice bowl for centuries.

Rice dominates Thai food to an extent that is sometimes difficult to appreciate for a Westerner. We have no staple, not even wheat, that comes anywhere close to it. In the Thai language, no-one ever talks simply of eating, the expression is to 'eat rice'. Although by no means does every recipe in this book have to be accompanied by it, no Thai would think of going for a whole day without a plate of rice. There is a well-known saying that 'a meal without rice leaves the stomach empty', and for a Thai this is absolutely true, in much the same way that a committed meat-eater would feel about a vegetarian meal.

Thai rice is justly famous, not only because of the scale of its production (it is one of the country's main exports), but because of its high quality. In the West we usually see the best of the crop, often sold under the name 'fragrant rice'. The Thai name is even more specific: *khao hom malii,* meaning 'jasmine-scented rice'. If you drive out of Bangkok even a short distance, or better still take a river boat, you can see just how much rice dominates the landscape of the Central Plains. There is nearly always some activity, depending on the season: the muddy fields may be being tilled (traditionally with water buffalo but usually nowadays with small mechanized tractors jokingly referred to as 'Japanese water buffalo'), or young shoots may be being transplanted, or groups of farmers may be harvesting. Close by the Chaophaya River the rice mills process the crop, and load it onto the deep, wide-bodied rice barges. Still made of wood, these great barges are strung together in trains behind a tugboat and towed downriver, their gunwales awash as the local river traffic of ferries and long-tailed boats churn up the water alongside.

By far the most usual way of eating rice is plain and steamed, eaten in spoonfuls with whatever accompanying dishes are on the table. The Thais eat most meals in shallow, Western-style plates, with a spoon and fork. There are, nevertheless, other Thai ways with rice, such as frying (*khao phad,* or fried rice, tastes best with leftover steamed rice from the day before), and boiling (to make the traditional breakfast dish *khao tom*). But by far the most common alternative treatment for rice, making virtually the second staple in Thailand, is in the form of noodles. *Kwitiaow,* as white rice noodles are called here and all over those Asian countries with a Chinese population, are very much a Chinese import, but from the earliest days of the settlement of Thailand; they probably came down with the slow migration of people from Yunnan. *Kwitiaow* are primarily for quick meals, and are a great lunchtime favourite.

Virtually all the populated parts of Thailand are peppered with noodle stalls; the noodles and other ingredients on display in glass cabinets. Rice noodles are either stir-fried or rapidly boiled in a soup. For the soup, which is, on the whole, more common, a handful of noodles are placed in a wire-mesh basket and dunked for a few seconds in a large pot of boiling water, then turned into a serving bowl. To these are added stock, chopped vegetables and any of a great variety of additions, from fish balls or pieces of liver to various meats, pre-cooked or just briefly dipped in the boiling water. Eaten dry, noodles are stir-fried with vegetables, seasoning and meats, often with just enough liquid to make a gravy.

LEFT *Harvesting shallots; they are used in great quantities in Thai cooking.*

RIGHT *Farmers take a break from the midday heat.*

TOP RIGHT *A farmer's house in the middle of fields of rice and other crops.*

KAENG KHIAO WAAN NEUA

Green beef curry

Definitely green, but rarely sweet, this is one of the basic Thai curry styles, and can be used with pork, chicken or duck as a variation from beef.

• SERVES FOUR •

5 cups/40 fl oz/1.25 ltr thin coconut milk
11 oz/300 g beef sirloin, cut into 1 × ¾ × ¼ in/
2.5 × 2 × 1 cm slices
2 tbsp fish sauce
½ tbsp palm sugar
10 small white aubergines (eggplants), quartered
3 fresh red chillies, quartered lengthwise
3 kaffir lime leaves, torn into small pieces
¼ cup/½ oz/15 g sweet basil leaves

CHILLI PASTE

20 fresh small green chillies, chopped roughly
1 tbsp sliced shallot
1 tbsp chopped garlic
1 tbsp sliced galangal (ka)
½ stalk of lemon grass, sliced
½ tbsp coriander seeds
2 tsp salt
1 tsp shrimp paste
½ tsp chopped kaffir lime zest
½ tsp chopped coriander root or stem
6 white peppercorns, crushed

Pound all the chilli paste ingredients except the green chillies together to form a fine paste, using a mortar and pestle or blender if you have one. Stir in green chillies.

Heat 1 cup/8 fl oz/225 ml of the coconut milk in a pan, add the chilli paste and cook for 2 minutes. Add the beef and the rest of the coconut milk, and bring to the boil. Add the fish sauce and palm sugar, boil for 2 more minutes, then add the aubergine and chilli and cook for 1 minute. Stir in the lime leaf, boil for 1 minute, add the basil and remove from the heat.

Serve in bowls accompanied by rice, pickled vegetables, salted eggs and sun-dried beef.

KAENG KAI

Red chicken curry

• SERVES SIX •

5 cups/40 fl oz/1.25 ltr thin coconut milk
1 quantity chilli paste (see choo chii kung, page 36)
10 white peppercorns, crushed
11 oz/300 g boneless skinned chicken breasts, cut across into
¼ in/5mm thick slices
3 tbsp fish sauce
½ tbsp palm sugar
7 small white aubergines (eggplants), quartered
3 fresh red chillies, quartered lengthwise
2 kaffir lime leaves, torn into small pieces
⅓ cup/¾ oz/20 g sweet basil leaves

Heat 1 cup/8 fl oz/225 ml of the coconut milk in a pan, stir in the chilli paste and white peppercorns, and cook for 2 minutes. Add the chicken slices, mix well and add the rest of the coconut milk. Bring to a boil, then add the fish sauce and palm sugar. Boil for 1 minute and then add the aubergine (eggplant), chilli and lime leaf. Bring back to the boil, cook for 3 minutes, add the basil, remove from the heat and serve.

Serve in bowls accompanied by rice, sun-dried beef, and salted preserved eggs.

Divide the basil and cabbage between the banana leaf squares or 6-8 ovenproof ramekins or cups. Top with the fish mixture and wrap up. Cook in a pressure cooker, or bake in a 350°F/180°C/gas 4 oven, covered in a pan half-filled with hot water, for 10 minutes.

Meanwhile, boil the remaining ½ cup/4 fl oz/100 ml of coconut milk in a pan, and add the cornflour (cornstarch) to thicken slightly.

After the fish mixture has cooked for 10 minutes, spoon the thickened coconut milk over the tops and sprinkle with the lime leaf and chilli. Pressure-cook or bake again for 5 more minutes. Stand for 5 minutes before serving.

Serve accompanied by rice.

HAW MOK PLAA

Steamed fish curry

Although curry is the closest English description, the final mixture is quite thick, and sets quite firmly in the steaming. The banana leaf wrapping not only makes the presentation attractive, but adds some flavour; nevertheless, it is not strictly necessary, and individual portions can be steamed in egg poaching cups.

• SERVES SIX–EIGHT •
11 oz/300 g fish fillets (flounder, sole or sea bass), skinned and cut into slices
2½ cups/20 fl oz/550 ml thin coconut milk
2 eggs, beaten
3 tbsp fish sauce
1 cup/2½ oz/60 g sweet basil leaves
1 cup/3 oz/75 g finely sliced cabbage
6 squares of banana leaf (optional)
1½ tbsp cornflour (cornstarch)
2 kaffir lime leaves, torn into small pieces
1 fresh red chilli, seeded and cut into strips
RED CURRY PASTE
10 small garlic cloves, chopped lightly
5 dried red chillies, chopped lightly
5 white peppercorns
3 shallots, chopped lightly
2 coriander roots, sliced
1 tsp sliced galangal (ka)
1 tsp chopped lemon grass
½ tsp finely chopped kaffir lime zest
½ tsp salt

Pound all the ingredients for the paste together with a mortar and pestle or in a blender until fine. Put in a bowl and stir in the fish pieces, and 2 cups/16 fl oz/450 ml of the coconut milk. Break in the eggs and mix well. Stir in the fish sauce.

KAENG KHUA SAPPAROD HOI MALAENG POO

Mussel and pineapple curry soup

• SERVES FOUR •
4½ cups/36 fl oz/1 ltr thin coconut milk
1 quantity chilli paste (see choo chii kung, page 36)
7 oz/200 g cooked mussel meat (steam approx. 1½ lb/675 g mussels in their shells and remove meat)
½ medium-sized pineapple, diced finely
1 kaffir lime leaf, torn into small pieces
2½ tbsp fish sauce
½ tbsp palm sugar

Heat a quarter of the coconut milk in a pan, add the chilli paste and cook for 2 minutes. Add the mussels, mix well, then add the rest of the ingredients and boil for 1 minute. Remove from the heat and serve.

Serve in bowls accompanied by rice.

TOM KHAA KAI

Coconut and galangal soup

This creamy soup has become one of the favourites on Thai restaurant menus, not least for the delicate aroma and flavour given by the galangal. Although rather like ginger in appearance, it is much milder and more fragrant.

• SERVES FOUR–SIX •
5 cups/40 fl oz/1.25 ltr thin coconut milk
1 oz/25 g shallot, chopped finely
½ oz/15 g galangal (ka), sliced thinly
2 stalks lemon grass, cut into ¾ in/2 cm pieces
6 fresh small whole red chillies
3 kaffir lime leaves, torn into small pieces
1 tsp salt
11 oz/300 g boneless skinned chicken breasts, cut across into
¼ in/5mm thick slices
7 oz/200 g fresh mushrooms, oyster if available
2 tbsp lime or lemon juice
½ tbsp fish sauce
3 tbsp coriander leaves and stems cut into ¾ in/2 cm pieces

Pour the coconut milk into a pan and bring to a boil. Add the shallot, galangal, lemon grass, chilli, lime leaf and salt. Boil, add the chicken and bring to the boil again, then add the mushrooms and bring back to the boil for 2 minutes. Remove from the heat and stir in the lime juice, fish sauce and coriander.

Serve in bowls accompanied by rice, lime quarters and phrik nam plaa (page 25).

KAENG CHEUD PLAA MUK

Stuffed squid soup

This is one of a range of clear, unspicy soups that are intended to accompany other dishes as a kind of mild counterpoint. 'Kaeng cheud' literally means 'plain soup', and at the table serves as a contrast to dishes that are either spicy or have oil.

• SERVES FOUR •
2 cups/12 oz/350 g minced (ground) pork
½ tsp white soya sauce
¼ tsp ground white pepper
11 oz/300 g squid, body not tentacles, cleaned
4 cups/32 fl oz/900 ml chicken stock
½ tbsp preserved cabbage, chopped roughly
7 white peppercorns, crushed
5 garlic cloves, crushed
1 tsp fish sauce
¼ tsp sugar
3 spring onions (scallions), cut into ½ in/1 cm pieces
2 tbsp coriander leaves and stems cut in ½ in/1 cm pieces

Mix the pork, soya sauce and white pepper together well and use to stuff the squid. If there is any extra pork mixture, form it into small meatballs.

Heat the chicken stock in a pan or wok, add the preserved cabbage, crushed peppercorns and garlic, and bring to a boil. Place the stuffed squid in the boiling stock, with meatballs if there are any, and then add the fish sauce and sugar. Boil until the stuffed squid is cooked, about 15 minutes or until it is no longer pink when cut into. Add the spring onion (scallion) and coriander and remove from the heat immediately.

Serve accompanied by rice.

TOM YUM KUNG

Hot and sour prawn (shrimp) soup

• SERVES FOUR •

3 cups/24 fl oz/675 ml chicken stock
3 stalks of lemon grass, cut into ¼ in/5 mm slices
3 kaffir lime leaves
12 raw medium-sized or 6 large prawns (shrimps), shelled
but not deheaded
5 oz/150 g mushrooms, halved
5 fresh small whole green chillies
¼ cup/¼ oz/10 g coriander leaves and stems, sliced
3 tbsp lime juice, or to taste
½ tbsp fish sauce, or to taste

Boil the stock in a pan, add the lemon grass and lime leaf, then the prawns (shrimps) and mushrooms. When the prawns (shrimps) are cooked, about 8–10 minutes, remove the pan from the heat and add the rest of the ingredients. Let stand for 5 minutes, then check the seasoning, adding more fish sauce or lime juice, or breaking up the chillies to release more heat as required – the soup should be spicy-sour and a little salty.

Serve accompanied by rice.

TOM KLONG PLAA KROB

Smoked fish soup

• SERVES FOUR–SIX •

4½ cups/36 fl oz/1 ltr chicken stock
½ oz/15 g galangal (ka), sliced
2 stalks of lemon grass, cut into 1½ in/4 cm pieces and
crushed lightly
1 tsp shrimp paste
9 oz/250 g dried smoked fish (not salted), bones removed
and broken into 3 or 4 pieces
1 oz/25 g shallot, crushed slightly
1½ tsp tamarind or lime juice, or to taste
½ cup/½ oz/15 g sweet basil leaves
1 tbsp fish sauce, or to taste
½ tsp salt
5 dried whole red chillies, dry-fried for 3-5 minutes

Pour the chicken stock into a pan, bring to a boil and add the galangal, lemon grass and shrimp paste. Boil again for 2 minutes and then add the dried fish pieces, shallot and tamarind juice. Bring back to a boil, and simmer for 5 minutes, then remove from the heat and add the rest of the ingredients. Mix and season to taste with more tamarind, lime juice or fish sauce if you like. Stand for 10 minutes before serving.

Serve accompanied by rice.

KWITIAOW PHAD THAI

Thai-fried noodles

The country's basic fried noodle dish. Quick and easy to prepare, it is usually eaten as a secondary rather than as a main dish.

• SERVES SIX •

½ cup/4 fl oz/100 ml peanut or corn oil
7 oz/200 g raw prawns (large shrimps), shelled
4 oz/100 g firm bean curd (tofu), diced
3 tbsp preserved sweet white radish, chopped
3 tbsp sliced shallots
4 eggs
11 oz/300 g rice or cellophane noodles (sen lek or woon sen),
soaked in cold water for 7-10 minutes, if dried
¼ cup/2 fl oz/50 ml chicken stock
3 tbsp dried shrimps, chopped
⅓ cup/2 oz/50 g unsalted peanuts, chopped
4 spring onions (scallions), sliced
15 oz/400 g bean sprouts

SAUCE
1 cup/8 fl oz/225 ml water
½ cup/4 fl oz/100 ml tamarind juice
⅓ cup/2 oz/50 g palm sugar
1 tbsp white soya sauce

Mix all the sauce ingredients together in a pan and boil until reduced to about ⅔ cup/5 fl oz/150 ml. Set aside to cool.

Heat the oil in a wok or pan until very hot, then add the prawns (shrimps) and bean curd and stir-fry lightly for 1 minute. Add the preserved radish and shallot, fry for 1 minute, and break in the eggs. Stir-fry for a minute, then add the noodles and chicken stock. When the noodles are soft (about 2 minutes), add the dried shrimps, peanuts, spring onions (scallions) and bean sprouts. Add the sauce, fry for a couple of minutes and serve.

Serve accompanied by chopped peanuts, chopped dry chillies, sugar, lime wedges, spring onions (scallions) and fresh bean sprouts, all in small saucers.

23

KHANOM CHIIN NAM YAA

White noodles with sauce

Rarely seen in restaurants, this is a very popular meal in itself. The basis is a folded nest of long white spaghetti-like rice noodles. The 'nam yaa' is the sauce. Because of their length, kanom chiin are commonly served at various ceremonies, including marriages: never broken until served, they signify long life. Although difficult to find freshly made in the West, dried khanom chiin are available (follow the cooking instructions on the packet), or substitute cooked spaghetti.

• SERVES FOUR–SIX •
7 oz/200 g sea bass, perch or white fish fillets, skinned
11 oz/300 g thin rice noodles (khanom chiin), soaked for 3 minutes if dried, or cooked spaghetti
6 cups/48 fl oz/1.35 ltr thin coconut milk
20 fish balls, frozen or bottled (optional)
3 tbsp fish sauce
4 oz/100 g bean sprouts, blanched
4 oz/100 g green (string) beans, cut into ½ in/1 cm lengths
4 oz/100 g morning glory (swamp cabbage), blanched
2 cups/5 oz/150 g lemon basil leaves
CHILLI PASTE
4 oz/100 g shallots, chopped finely
2 oz/50 g garlic cloves, chopped
2 oz/50 g dried salted mackerel or other fish, chopped lightly
1 cup/8 fl oz/225 ml water
1 cup/6 oz/175 g sliced krachai
2 tbsp sliced lemon grass
4 dried red chillies, seeded
2 tsp sliced galangal (ka)
1 tsp shrimp paste
1tsp salt

Mix all the chilli paste ingredients together, put in a pan or wok and cook over medium heat for 1 minute. Cool and then chop in a blender or food processor. Put to one side.

Boil fish in a small amount of water for 10 minutes. Remove,

cool slightly and chop finely (or process quickly in a food processor). Boil the noodles quickly for 5 minutes, drain, cool and place in serving bowls.

Heat the coconut milk in a pan, add the chilli paste mixture, the fish and the fish balls if using, the fish sauce, and boil for 3 minutes. Remove from the heat.

Top the noodles with the fish mixture. Arrange the bean sprouts, beans, morning glory and lemon basil around the side.

KHAO THANG NAA THANG

Rice crackers with pork and coconut sauce

• SERVES FOUR–SIX •
3 cups/1¼ lb/550 g cooked rice
approx. 3 cups/24 fl oz/675 ml peanut or corn oil for deep-frying
1 tsp chopped coriander root
1 tsp chopped garlic
2 cups/16 fl oz/450 ml thin coconut milk
¾ cup/5 oz/150 g cooked pork, chopped
¾ cup/5 oz/150 g raw shelled small shrimps, chopped
1 tsp lightly chopped coriander leaf and stem
1 fresh red chilli, cut into lengthwise strips
1 cup/5 oz/150 g unsalted peanuts, chopped small
2 tbsp sliced shallots
¼ tsp ground white pepper
½ tbsp palm sugar
1 tsp salt

Knead the rice slightly until it is sticky, then press it onto a slightly oiled non-stick baking pan in a layer ⅛ in/5 mm thick. Place in the sun for 1–2 days or in a warm (325°F/ 170°C) oven until very dry, 3–5 hours. Then, remove the rice from the pan and break it into 2 in/5 cm pieces.

Heat the oil in a wok or pan to a temperature of 350°F/ 180°C. Fry the rice crackers until a light tan colour, 3–5 minutes. Remove them with a slotted spoon and drain well on kitchen paper (paper towel).

To make the sauce, pound the coriander root and garlic together in a pestle and mortar. Heat the coconut milk in a pan and add the coriander and garlic mixture. Bring to the boil, add the pork, shrimps and remaining ingredients, and continue to boil until the meat is cooked, about 7–10 minutes. Remove the pan from the heat, pour into a bowl and sprinkle with the coriander leaf and chilli.

Serve the sauce with the rice crackers.

KOP PHAD PHED

Spicy-fried frogs' legs

• SERVES FOUR •

⅓ cup/3 fl oz/75 ml peanut or corn oil
2 tbsp red chilli paste (bottled, or see kaeng ped yang,
page 50)
8 sets frogs' legs
2 oz/50 g green peppercorns
5 small white aubergines (eggplants), quartered
3 fresh red chillies, sliced lengthwise
¼ cup/1½ oz/40 g galangal (ka) or ginger, cut into fine
matchsticks
2 tsp fish sauce
½ tsp palm sugar
⅓ cup/¾ oz/20 g sweet basil leaves

Heat the oil in a wok or pan, add the chilli paste and fry for
2 minutes, then mix in the frogs' legs and peppercorns. Add
the aubergine (eggplant), chilli, galangal or ginger, fish
sauce and sugar, mix well and fry for 3 minutes. Stir in the
basil and take off the heat.

Serve accompanied by rice.

YAM MA MUANG

Green mango salad

A bit sour for some people, you can add more sugar to this salad
if you like.

• SERVES FOUR •

2 cups/12 oz/350 g green unripe mango flesh, cut into
long matchsticks
¼ cup/1 oz/25 g unsweetened grated coconut, dry-fried until
light brown
¼ cup/1 oz/25 g dried shrimps
3 tbsp sliced shallots
5 fresh small green chillies, chopped
1 tbsp palm sugar, or to taste
fish sauce, to taste (optional)
lime juice, to taste (optional)

Mix all the ingredients together. If not salty enough add a
little fish sauce; if not sour enough, add lime juice.

PHRIK NAM PLAA

Fish sauce with chillies

This spicy sauce is found on all Thai tables and is used to add
both spiciness and saltiness to dishes.

¼ cup/2 fl oz/50 ml fish sauce
10 fresh small green chillies, sliced into small circles
1 tsp sliced shallot
¼ tsp palm sugar
1 tbsp lime or lemon juice

Mix all the ingredients together well. This is good for
accompanying almost all Thai food, especially rice. Just
sprinkle a little on your food to liven it up.

NAM PHRIK PLA TOO

Spicy dip with mackerel

• SERVES SIX •

3 × 4 oz/100 g baby mackerel, cleaned and gutted, or
1½ tsp salt
11 oz/300 g boneless mackerel fillets
½ tbsp shrimp paste
2 tbsp dried shrimps, pounded fine
1 tbsp sliced garlic
2 small green aubergines (eggplants), peeled
15 fresh small whole green or red chillies
6 pea-sized aubergines (eggplants) or fresh green peas
2 tbsp lemon juice
1 tbsp fish sauce
½ tbsp palm sugar
1 fresh large red chilli, sliced into small circles
¼ cup/2 fl oz/50 ml peanut or corn oil

Rub the mackerel inside and out with the salt and leave in a cool place for 1 hour.

Dry-fry the shrimp paste in foil over high heat for 5 minutes (or roast in a 350°F/180°C/gas 4 oven for 8 minutes), then unwrap. Pound the shrimp paste, dried shrimp, garlic and aubergine (eggplant) together with a mortar and pestle or in a blender. Add the small chillies, pound lightly, then thoroughly mix in the rest of the ingredients except the red chilli slices, which are sprinkled on top as a garnish.

Heat the oil in a frying pan (skillet) or wok over medium heat and fry the fish for 6-8 minutes on each side – the flesh should be tender but firm and white at the centre.

Serve accompanied by fresh vegetables, such as lightly boiled cabbage and green (string) beans.

GLUAI TOD

Fried bananas

If at all possible, buy small, fragrant bananas for this (and other) banana desserts.

• SERVES FOUR–SIX •
3 cups / 12 oz / 350 g rice flour
1 cup / 8 fl oz / 225 ml water
½ cup / 2 oz / 50 g unsweetened grated coconut
3 tbsp plain (all-purpose) flour
3 tbsp sugar
2 tbsp sesame seeds
2 tsp baking powder
1 tsp salt
approx. 6 cups / 48 fl oz / 1.35 ltr peanut or corn oil for deep-frying
1 lb / 450 g small, slightly green bananas, quartered

Mix together well in a bowl all the ingredients except the oil and bananas. Heat the oil in a wok or deep pan to about 350°F/180°C.

Dip the banana pieces into the coconut batter and then deep-fry until brown but not dark, about 3 minutes. Turn over and cook for 2 more minutes. Take out with a slotted spoon and drain on kitchen paper (paper towel).

Serve immediately as dessert.

SANGKHYAA FAK THONG

Coconut custard in young pumpkin

This is a special – and to my mind, more interesting – version of one of the best-known and most well-loved Thai desserts. Although more usually served in a coconut shell, a hollowed pumpkin not only looks more attractive, but its flesh gives a pleasing contrast to the sweet custard.

• SERVES FOUR–SIX •
1 small pumpkin
9 duck or chicken eggs
1½ cups / 10 oz / 275 g palm sugar
2 cups / 16 fl oz / 450 ml thin coconut milk

Slice off and remove the top of the pumpkin carefully and clean out the seeds thoroughly. Whisk the eggs, sugar and coconut milk together in a bowl until frothy, and allow to stand for 10 minutes. Then, strain through muslin into the pumpkin.

Steam for 30 minutes in a covered wok or steamer with the pumpkin lid steamed on the side: the custard is cooked when a skewer comes out clean. Cool overnight in the refrigerator. Replace the pumpkin lid before serving, then cut into wedges to eat.

FOI THONG

Gold threads

• SERVES SIX •
4 egg shells
6 cups/2 lb 2 oz/1 kg sugar
8 cups/64 fl oz/1.8 ltr water
1 tsp vanilla essence or jasmine water
15 egg yolks, duck if available, whisked lightly

Take a metal cup measure or a well washed empty can and punch about 25 small holes into its base with a nail or punch. Wash well.

Put the egg shells, sugar and water in a pan, bring to a boil and simmer until reduced by about half. Strain the liquid through cheesecloth.

Bring the strained syrup back to a simmer, and add the essence. Then, pour the whisked egg yolks through the 'strainer' over the simmering sugar syrup (cook in batches of about ½ can at a time). Let cook for 1 minute and remove with a slotted spoon or strainer. Repeat the process until all the egg is used, placing the threads on a rack to drain. When cool, gather into small bundles and serve or refrigerate until ready to use.

KHANOM PIAK POON

Sweet blackened jelly

This unusual dessert must be one of the few dishes anywhere in the world that makes use of the outside of a mature coconut – something that, fortunately, is usually readily available in the West!

• S E R V E S   S I X – E I G H T •

½ cup/12 oz/50 g coconut hair (hairy brown coating from outside of coconuts)
6 cups/48 fl oz/1.35 ltr water
3 cups/12 oz/350 g rice flour
½ tbsp tapioca flour
2½ cups/1 lb/450 g palm sugar
2½ cups/10 oz/275 g unsweetened grated coconut
¼ tsp salt

Take the coconut hair and roast it in a 375°F/190°C/gas 5 oven for about 20 minutes until black, stirring occasionally, then chop well. Mix it with 1 cup/8 fl oz/225 ml of the water and then strain twice through muslin.

Put both the flours in a large bowl, mix well, then stir in the remaining water and the sugar. Stir in the cup of black water mixture and strain again through cloth.

Place the liquid in a stainless steel pan and slowly bring to a boil, stirring constantly, for about 20 minutes, until very thick – don't burn the bottom. When thick, pour into ungreased shallow cake pans and leave to cool for 1 hour. Refrigerate for 1 hour or overnight.

To remove the jelly, warm the pans by dipping them in warm water and then inverting onto a plate. Cut the jelly into bite-sized pieces. Mix the coconut with the salt and sprinkle over the top.

KHAO NIAOW MA MUANG

Sticky rice with mangoes

A simple dessert (once you have mastered the steaming of sticky rice, see page 15), but always successful. It works because of contrasts: in flavour between the sweetness of the coconut milk and the yellow Thai mango, and in texture between the rice and the mango.

• S E R V E S   F O U R – S I X •

2 cups/1 lb/450 g sticky rice
3½ cups/28 fl oz/775 ml thin coconut milk
⅓ cup/2 oz/50 g sugar
½ tsp salt
½ tsp cornflour (cornstarch)
2 ripe mangoes, peeled and sliced

Soak the rice in water for 4 hours, rinse well 3 times in lukewarm water and drain very well. Line a strainer with cheesecloth, add the rice and place over a pan of boiling water – don't let the water touch the bottom of the rice. Cover and steam for about 30 minutes until fairly soft.

Mix 3 cups/24 fl oz/675 ml of the coconut milk with the sugar and ¼ tsp of the salt. Stir in the rice and mix well.

Mix the remaining ½ cup/4 fl oz/100 ml of coconut milk with the ¼ tsp salt and the cornflour (cornstarch) together in a small pan, bring to a boil, simmer for 2 minutes and cool.

Place the sticky rice onto serving plates, spoon the cornflour sauce over the top and arrange the mango slices around the edges.

THONG YOD

Golden balls

• SERVES SIX •

20 egg yolks, duck if available
4 cups/1 lb/450 g rice flour
8 cups/64 fl oz/1.8 ltr water
6 cups/2 lb 2 oz/1 kg sugar
4 egg shells
1 tsp jasmine water or vanilla essence

Mix the egg yolks well with the flour in a bowl and put to one side. Boil the water and sugar in a pan with the egg shells until reduced to about half, then strain through muslin, put back in the pan and bring back to simmer. Add the jasmine or vanilla essence.

Take pieces of the egg mixture and form balls the size of large round grapes. Place them in the simmering sugar syrup; cook until they float to the surface, then remove with a slotted spoon and drain on kitchen paper (paper towel). Strain the syrup again through cloth into a large bowl and leave to cool.

Soak the cooked balls in the strained syrup for 30 minutes, then remove them with a slotted spoon and refrigerate. Serve when cool.

MET KANOON

Jackfruit seeds

These candies are one of a range of Thai sweetmeats made with egg yolks. Kanoon, or jackfruit, is not used in the recipe – they are only called after the fruit because of the similar shape.

• SERVES SIX–EIGHT •

2 cups/12 oz/350 g dried yellow mung beans
5 cups/1 lb/12 oz/875 g sugar
4 cups/32 fl oz/900 ml thin coconut milk
5 cups/40 fl oz/1.25 ltr water
10 egg yolks, duck if possible, whisked lightly

Soak the mung beans in water for 1 hour, then drain and steam them for 20 minutes or until soft. Mash or purée in a food processor.

Put the beans in a pan with 2 cups/12 oz/350 g of the sugar and the coconut milk. Bring to a boil and then simmer, stirring, until reduced to a paste, about 15 minutes – be careful not to burn the mixture. Remove from the heat and leave to cool.

Meanwhile, make the syrup: boil the water with the remaining sugar until reduced by half. Remove 1 cup/8 fl oz/225 ml of the syrup and put to one side. Keep the remaining syrup simmering slowly.

Take pieces of the bean paste and shape them into small fingertip-sized ovals. Cook them in batches of 8–10 at a time: dip first into the egg yolk and then into the pan of syrup. Wait until they float to the top, then remove with a slotted spoon and drain on kitchen paper (paper towel). Place them in the reserved cup of syrup for 30 minutes, remove and allow to dry for 5 minutes.

Serve immediately or cover and refrigerate; serve at room temperature.

GLUAI BUAD CHII

Banana cooked in coconut milk

The addition of a little salt gives a refreshing and slightly unusual flavour. This dessert goes well with ice cream.

• SERVES FOUR •
2–3 small, slightly green bananas
4 cups/32 fl oz/900 ml thin coconut milk
1 cup/6 oz/175 g sugar
1/4 tsp salt

Slice the bananas lengthwise, then in half. Pour the coconut milk into a pan, add the sugar and salt. Bring to a boil, add the bananas, bring back to the boil for 2 minutes and then remove from the heat. Serve with the coconut milk.

Serve hot or cold.

THE GULF OF THAILAND

If the wide plains of the Menam Chaophaya are the country's rice bowl, the great gulf into which the river flows is the source of Thailand's protein. Night and day, from ports strung along the coast on either side of the delta, the fishing fleets of brightly painted wooden trawlers set out to fish the rice waters of what the Thais call 'Ao Thai'. The country's fishing industry is one of South-east Asia's largest, and brings in a huge haul of mackerel, mullet, cobia, amberjack and many other species (fish, unfortunately, are not the only catch: some Thai fishermen also have a reputation for part-time piracy).

Prachuap Khiri Khan on the coast of the narrow Isthmus of Kra is typical of the small gulf ports. For much of the day the long jetty lies silent in the stifling heat, but when the fleet is in, and especially at night, it swarms with people, offloading the catch, hosing down decks, winching huge blocks of ice down into the holds, repairing nets. By morning, the fish will be in the markets, and shortly after that cooked in any number of ways in homes and restaurants.

The fish population of the Gulf of Thailand, and of the Andaman Sea across the isthmus leading down to Malaysia, is understandably rather different from the catches we are used to seeing in Europe and America. Nevertheless, there are substitutes for all of the popular species, and even though you might not be able to make an exactly authentic match, this is not so important. What does matter is to make sure that the flesh of whatever fish you choose has similar characteristics to the Thai fish used in a particular dish. For instance, if you are cooking *plaa raad phrik,* the flesh should be firm, so that the fish retains its shape. A Thai cook would probably use *plaa kapong.* In Northern Europe sea perch would do as well, and in North America, sea bass.

In some Western cities it may be possible to buy Asian fish that have been deep-frozen. Whether you use this or a local catch depends very much on how much you value freshly-caught fish. Also remember that with steamed dishes, the flavour of the fish will come through much more with the spicier preparations, so fresh is preferable.

The following are among the most popular fishes used by Thais:
Plaa chorn A popular fish, known in English as cobia, runner or blackfish. The flesh is white, firm, with a good flavour. It resembles Spanish mackerel.
Paa duk Catfish.
Plaa jaramet Pomfret (or ray's bream), a medium-sized, silvery deep-bodied but thin fish. Highly regarded in South-east Asia because of its exquisite taste, the white, firm flesh comes away easily from the bones, making it good for *plaa jian.*
Plaa kabork Grey mullet or snapper; a small to medium-sized fish.
Plaa kapong This common fish name covers a number of species of both snapper and perch. The eating quality of the different types varies, a fact that the sharper Thai fish-sellers take full advantage of. One of the tastiest varieties is the Thai sea perch; the nearest equivalent in Northern Europe and North America is local sea perch or sea bass.
Plaa karang Grouper, a firm, white delicate fish that is highly prized. Found in various colours.
Plaa pan Pony fish.

Plaa samlii Amberjack, kingfish or cottonfish.

In addition to fish, the seafood catch also includes shrimps, prawns, crabs and other shellfish.

By no means all of the Gulf's rich fish is cooked. In the tropics, the traditional solution to the problem of preserving fish that cannot be eaten right away is fermentation. In Europe and America, the old methods are salting and drying, but in the hot, humid climate of Thailand there is a much higher risk of the fish going rotten. Nowadays, ice and refrigerated trucks make this no real problem, but the taste for fermented fish is deeply ingrained. One of the most popular ingredients in, and accompaniments to, Thai food is the slightly pungent, salty brown liquid known as *nam plaa,* fish sauce. At its finest quality a clear amber colour, it is virtually identical to *nuoc mam* in Vietnam and other similar sauces used throughout Southeast Asia. Although the idea of a foodstuff made from fermented fish may sound less than appealing to many Westerners, there is no hint at all of rotteness; *nam plaa* gives one of the characteristic and unreproduceable flavours to Thai food.

In its use, *nam plaa* is universal, and can be made from sea or freshwater fish. Commercially, most is made close to the Gulf, and the best-known centre of production is Rayong, a seaport a little way beyond Pattaya on the road that runs east from Bangkok. Here, tons of fish from the daily catch brought in by the fleet of trawlers are converted into sauce. Layers of fish and salt are alternated in large vats, pressed down and allowed to stand for a few months. The liquid from this fermentation is then drawn off and bottled; lesser quality sauce comes from the addition of more salt water (rather like second and third pressings of olive oil). The *nam plaa* is then natured in the bottles – traditionally in earthenware jars – and sold (see page 14 for more details of nam plaa's usage).

LEFT *Fishing boats in Hua Hin, whose catch is sold all over the country, including at the local market* (ABOVE).

PLAA RAAD PHRIK

Fried fish topped with chilli sauce

The scoring makes small trenches in the flesh for the sauce, which is not intended to surround the fish, but to be poured on top at the last minute.

• SERVES FOUR–SIX •
8 garlic cloves
5 fresh yellow chillies
2¼ lb/1 kg whole perch or sea bass, cleaned and gutted
approx. 3 cups/24 fl oz/675 ml peanut or corn oil for frying
½ tsp each salt and ground white pepper
plain (all-purpose) flour for dusting
½ cup/4 fl oz/100 ml chicken stock
2 fresh red chillies, quartered lengthwise
1 tbsp tamarind juice or vinegar
2 tsp sugar
1 tsp fish sauce
½ cup/½ oz/15 g sweet basil leaves, fried in oil for 1 minute until crisp

Pound the garlic and chilli together lightly with a mortar and pestle or in a blender.

Score the fish on both sides 5–6 times, sprinkle on the salt and pepper and dust with flour. Heat the oil to 350°F/180°C in a pan or wok and fry the fish well, until crisp but tender inside, about 7–10 minutes. Remove and drain the fish and put in a serving dish.

Take out all except approx. ¼ cup/2 fl oz/50 ml of the oil. Then, cook the garlic and chilli mixture, add the rest of the ingredients (except for the basil) and boil lightly for about 5 minutes until slightly thick. Pour on top of the fish and sprinkle over the fried basil to garnish.

Serve accompanied by rice.

PLAA PHAO

Grilled (broiled) whole fish

This straightforward treatment is given added interest, in Thai fashion, by the nam chim sauce served as an accompaniment.

• SERVES FOUR •
12 garlic cloves, crushed
5 coriander roots
2 tbsp brandy
1 tbsp white peppercorns, crushed
2 tsp white soya sauce
2 small whole (1 lb 6 oz/600 g each) sea bass, perch or cotton fish, cleaned and gutted
1 tsp salt
fresh banana leaves or foil squares for wrapping
butter for greasing
NAM CHIM SAUCE
¼ cup/2 fl oz/50 ml tamarind, lime or lemon juice
2 tbsp fish sauce
2 tbsp sliced shallots
1 tbsp palm sugar
1 tsp finely sliced fresh small green chilli
1 tsp finely chopped coriander leaf and stem

Pound the garlic, coriander root, brandy, white peppercorns and soya sauce together with a pestle and mortar or in a blender. Rub the fish with salt and then with the garlic mixture.

Grease the banana leaves or squares of foil with butter and 1 tsp water and use to wrap each fish individually. Roast in a 350°F/180°C/gas 4 oven or grill (broil) under medium heat for approx. 15–20 minutes until cooked, turning over once.

Meanwhile, mix all the ingredients for the nam chim sauce together well. When the fish are cooked, remove them from their wrappings and serve with the sauce.

Serve accompanied by rice.

PLAA NUNG MANAO PHRIK SOD

Steamed fish with lemon and chilli

The combination of lemon or lime juice and fresh chillies in the topping give this dish a refreshing spicy tartness.

• SERVES FOUR •

1 lb 2 oz/500 g whole sea bass or sea perch, cleaned and gutted
½ cup/4 fl oz/100 ml lemon or lime juice
2 tbsp lightly chopped fresh small green chillies
2 tbsp chopped garlic
2 tbsp fish sauce
½ tbsp salt
1 tsp sugar
¼ cup/¼ oz/10 g coriander leaves and stems, cut into ½ in/1 cm pieces

Steam the fish whole for 15 minutes until tender but firm. Meanwhile, mix all the remaining ingredients except the coriander together. When the fish is cooked, place it on a serving platter and spread the lemon juice mixture all over (the fish must be very hot when the sauce is poured over). Sprinkle with the coriander and serve.

Serve accompanied by rice.

KHAO PHAD KUNG

Shrimp-fried rice

• SERVES SIX •

½ cup/4 fl oz/100 ml peanut or corn oil
1 tbsp chopped garlic
7 oz/200 g raw shelled shrimps
3 eggs, beaten
⅓ cup/1½ oz/40 g sliced onion
1 tomato, cut into 6 pieces
4 cups/1¾ lb/750 g cooked rice
⅛ cup/½ oz/15 g chopped spring onion (scallion)
½ tbsp white soya sauce
1 tsp sugar
1 tsp salt
1 tsp ground white pepper
½ cup/2 oz/50 g cucumber, peeled and sliced into circles

Heat the oil in a wok or pan and add the garlic. Stir-fry and then add the shrimps and fry for 1 minute. Add the eggs and cook for another minute, stirring well, then add the onion and tomato. Stir-fry for 1 minute then add the rice, spring onion (scallion), soya sauce, sugar, salt and pepper. Stir well over a high heat for 3 minutes. Scoop onto serving plates and arrange the cucumber pieces around.

Serve accompanied by phrik nam plaa sauce (page 25), and eat with whole spring onions (scallions) and raw sliced cucumber.

KUNG KRATHIAM PHRIK THAI

Prawns (shrimps) fried with garlic and pepper

• SERVES FOUR •

approx. ½ cup/4 fl oz/100 ml peanut or corn oil for frying
11 oz/300 g raw prawns (large shrimps), shelled
½ tbsp lightly chopped garlic
2 tbsp ground white pepper
1 tsp salt

Heat the oil in a pan or wok, add the prawns (shrimps) and brown lightly for about 2 minutes. Remove all but a quarter of the oil and add the garlic, pepper and salt to the prawns (shrimps) in the pan. Fry lightly for 2 more minutes until brown. Drain off most of the remaining oil and serve immediately.

Serve accompanied by rice and sliced cucumber.

PO TAEK

Seafood soup

The seafood ingredients that I have listed here are only suggestions. Use whatever is available at the fishmongers, but try to assemble a variety of textures and flavours: the more the better.

• SERVES FOUR–SIX •
6 cups/48 fl oz/1.35 ltr chicken stock
5 oz/150 g sea bass or other firm fish, cleaned, gutted and cut into 6 pieces
5 raw prawns (large shrimps), shelled
1 blue crab, cleaned, shell removed and chopped into 6 pieces
6 mussels in their shells, cleaned well
5 oz/150 g squid, body and tentacles, cleaned, gutted and cut into 3/4 in/2 cm pieces
2 stalks of lemon grass, cut into 2 in/5 cm lengths and crushed
1/4 cup/1 1/2 oz/40 g sliced galangal (ka)
3 kaffir lime leaves, shredded
1/2 cup/1/2 oz/15 g sweet basil leaves
8 fresh small green chillies, crushed lightly
5 dried red chillies, fried lightly
2 1/2 tbsp fish sauce, or to taste
1/4 tsp palm sugar
1 tbsp lime or lemon juice, or to taste

Pour the chicken stock into a wok or pan, bring to a boil and add all the fish and seafood. Then add the lemon grass, galangal and lime leaf. Boil, add all the rest of the ingredients, cook for 2 more minutes, and remove from the heat. Taste and add more fish sauce or lime juice as it pleases you.

Serve in bowls accompanied by rice, fish sauce and lime or lemon juice.

CHOO CHII KUNG

Prawns (shrimps) with coconut milk and chilli paste

• SERVES FOUR •
2 cups/16 fl oz/450 ml thin coconut milk
1 lb/450 g raw prawns (large shrimps), shelled
2 tbsp fish sauce
1 1/2 tbsp sugar
2 fresh large red chillies, cut into matchsticks
1 tbsp coriander leaves
1 tsp shredded kaffir lime leaf
CHILLI PASTE
5 dried red chillies, chopped roughly
1 1/2 tbsp sliced shallot
1/2 tbsp finely sliced lemon grass
1/2 tbsp chopped garlic
2 tsp salt
1 tsp shrimp paste
1 tsp sliced galangal (ka)
1/2 tsp chopped kaffir lime zest
1/2 tsp chopped coriander root or stem

Pound all the chilli paste ingredients together with a mortar and pestle or in a blender to form a fine paste.

Heat 1 cup/8 fl oz/225 ml of the coconut milk in a pan or wok, add the chilli paste and fry for 2–3 minutes until fragrant. Add the prawns (shrimps) and fry for 1 minute, then add the rest of the coconut milk, the fish sauce and palm sugar. Boil for 2 minutes, then remove from the heat. Transfer to a serving bowl and garnish with the coriander, chilli and lime leaf.

Serve accompanied by rice.

YAM THALAE

Spicy seafood salad

The Thai versions of salad, of which this is one, are flavourful assemblies of different ingredients quite unlike those we are accustomed to in the West. Most are extremely spicy. This 'yam' combines three of the basic five flavours: spicy, sour and salty.

• SERVES SIX •

5 oz/150 g sea bass or perch, cleaned, gutted and sliced thinly into strips
5 oz/150 g prawns (large shrimps), shelled
5 oz/150 g squid, body and tentacles, cleaned, gutted and sliced into ¾ in/2 cm strips
7 fresh small green chillies
5 garlic cloves
2 coriander roots
2 tbsp fish sauce
½ tsp sugar
2 tbsp lime or lemon juice
4 spring onions (scallions), sliced into ¼ in/5 mm pieces
4 oz/100 g onions, sliced thinly
2 oz/50 g celery leaves and stems, sliced

Cook the fish, prawns (shrimps) and squid separately in salted water until cooked, about 2–3 minutes each, and drain.

Pound the chillies, garlic, coriander root, fish sauce and sugar together with a pestle and mortar or in a blender until fine. Place in a bowl and mix in the lemon juice, spring onion (scallion), onion and celery. Stir in the fish and seafood and mix well. Serve immediately.

YAM HOI MALAENG POO

Spicy mussel salad

• SERVES FOUR •

15 oz/400 g cooked mussel meat (steam approx. 3½ lb/1.5 kg mussels in their shells and remove meat)
10 fresh small green chillies, chopped finely
¼ cup/¼ oz/10 g mint leaves
3 tbsp lime or lemon juice, or to taste
2½ tbsp fish sauce, or to taste
2 tbsp sliced shallots
2 tbsp ginger cut into matchsticks
2 tbsp finely sliced lemon grass
½ tbsp shredded kaffir lime leaf
1 small head of white Chinese cabbage, cut into wedges
½ small head of green cabbage, cut into wedges

Mix together all the ingredients except the cabbage in a bowl. Taste for seasoning, adding extra lime juice or fish sauce if you like. Serve on a platter, with the cabbage leaves around the edge to be eaten with the salad.

HOI LAI PHAD PHRIK PAO

Baby clams with chilli and basil

You can also use cockles or larger clams for this dish; just increase the cooking time a little.

• **SERVES FOUR** •

approx. ⅓ cup/3 fl oz/75 ml peanut or corn oil for frying
1 lb 6 oz/600 g fresh baby clams in their shells, cleaned well
1½ tbsp chopped garlic
5 fresh red chillies, sliced lengthwise
2 tbsp red chilli paste
2 tsp white soya sauce
½ cup/4 fl oz/100 ml chicken stock
1 cup/2½ oz/60 g sweet basil leaves

Heat the oil in a pan or wok until quite hot, about 375°F/190°C. Add the clams and garlic, and cook until the clams open slightly, 2–3 minutes. Add the fresh chillies, chilli paste, and soya sauce, mix well, then pour in the chicken stock. Bring to a boil, cook for 2 minutes, stir in the basil and serve immediately.

Serve accompanied by rice.

HOI SHELL

Thai-style scallops

A great favourite, and an especially tasty alternative to normally bland treatments for this shellfish.

• **SERVES FOUR** •

16 medium-sized scallops, with 4 shells if available
2 oz/50 g butter, melted
2 tbsp lime juice
1 tbsp chopped garlic
1 tbsp chopped shallot
1 tbsp chopped ginger
1 tbsp chopped coriander leaf
salt and ground white pepper to taste

Mix the scallops with all the other ingredients in a bowl, and season. If you have the scallop shells, place 4 scallops with mixture in each shell; otherwise put all in a heatproof dish.

Bake in a 350°F/180°C/gas 4 oven or grill (broil) under medium heat until just cooked, about 10 minutes. Do not overcook.

Serve with other dishes or double the recipe and serve with rice.

HOI TOD

Fried mussel pancakes

Mussels and pancakes may seem an unlikely combination, but here the batter is made from tapioca flour. This is essentially market food – if you stroll through the night market of any provincial town you can hear, and smell, the sizzling of this dish.

• **MAKES EIGHT** •

1 cup/8 fl oz/225 ml peanut or corn oil for frying
2 cups/12 oz/350 g raw mussel or oyster meat
8 eggs
11 oz/300 g large bean sprouts
3 tbsp finely sliced spring onions (scallions)
2 tsp ground white pepper
BATTER
2 cups/16 fl oz/450 ml water
½ cup/2 oz/50 g plain (all-purpose) flour
1 cup/4 oz/100 g tapioca flour or cornflour (cornstarch)
2 tbsp baking powder
2 tbsp sugar
2 eggs, beaten
2 tsp salt

Mix all the batter ingredients together thoroughly (alternatively, use store-bought tempura batter). Heat a large, heavy frying pan or skillet, preferably cast iron, and add about ½ in/1 cm oil.

Mix ¼ cup/1½ oz/40 g of the mussel meat and ¼ cup/2 fl oz/50 ml of the batter together and pour into the pan. Cook over medium heat for about 5 minutes until brown on the bottom, then break one egg on top of the mussel cake. Flip over carefully and fry until the egg is lightly browned, 3–5 minutes. Remove the mussel cake from the pan and drain well on kitchen paper (paper towel). Repeat with the rest of the mussel and batter to make 8 cakes.

Add the bean sprouts to the pan and fry lightly. Place on a serving plate, and arrange the mussel cakes on top. Sprinkle with the spring onion (scallion) and white pepper before serving.

Serve accompanied by Siricha chilli sauce or other thick chilli or hot sauce.

POO JAA

Stuffed crab shells

This dish is as well-known in Thailand for its name as for anything else – it means, literally, 'dear crab', for reasons which no-one has ever been able to explain convincingly.

• SERVES FOUR •
4 blue crab shells, cleaned well
3 eggs, beaten well
approx. 5 cups/40 fl oz/1.25 ltr peanut or corn oil for deep-frying
1/4 cup/1/4 oz/10 g coriander leaves
2 fresh red chillies, cut into lengthwise strips
STUFFING
1 cup/6 oz/175 g cooked minced (ground) pork
1/2 cup/3 oz/75 g minced (ground) shrimps or prawns
1/3 cup/2 1/2 oz/60 g crab meat, fresh or drained very well if canned
2 tbsp finely chopped onion
1 tbsp finely sliced spring onion (scallion)
1 tsp ground white pepper
1 tsp sugar
1/4 tsp white soya sauce
1/4 tsp salt

Mix all the stuffing ingredients together and fill the crab shells. Heat the oil in a pan or wok to approx. 350°F/180°C.

Dip the stuffed crabs in the beaten egg to coat them well all over and then deep-fry until thoroughly cooked, about 10–15 minutes. Remove and drain well on kitchen paper (paper towel). Sprinkle with the coriander and chilli before serving. Serve as an hors d'oeuvre or with rice and bottled Chinese plum sauce.

POO PHAD PONG KARII

Crab with curry powder

As you will probably have realized by now, spicy heat in Thai food is provided by chillies. Here, curry powder is used for its flavour, and the dish is not, by Thai standards, hot.

• SERVES FOUR–SIX •
1/4 cup/2 fl oz/50 ml peanut or corn oil
1 tbsp chopped garlic
1–2 whole blue crabs in shells (1 lb 10 oz/700 g each), cleaned and cut through shell into 4–6 pieces
1 tbsp curry powder
3 fresh red chillies, cut into lengthwise strips
1/2 cup/2 oz/50 g celery leaves and stem, cut into 3/4 in/2 cm pieces
4 spring onions (scallions), cut into 3/4 in/2 cm pieces
1/2 tsp white soya sauce

Heat the oil in a wok or pan, add the garlic and crab pieces, mix well, cook for 1 minute and then stir in the curry powder. Stir-fry for a minute, add the chilli; stir-fry for another minute and add the celery, spring onion (scallion) and soya sauce; then stir-fry again for about 2 minutes. If the pan gets too dry add a couple of tbsp of water.

Serve accompanied by rice.

BANGKOK

Thailand was always a rural country – rice fields, hamlets and villages still make up the typical landscape. Even the capital, Bangkok, was for more than a century little more than an extended conglomeration of villages. Away from the Royal Palace, government buildings and the Westernized houses of the foreign residents and richer Thai families, there was little to distinguish the local communities around the canals and lanes from any other settlement in this part of the country.

Now, however, Bangkok is booming, and at an accelerating pace. A decade ago, the Temple of the Golden Mount dominated the skyline of a large part of the city, as it was intended to do. Now, high-rise office blocks, shopping centres, hotels and condominiums are going up as fast as the construction industry can build them. Most of the city's famous canals have been filled in to make streets and roads that are woefully inadequate for Bangkok's horrendous traffic.

Many people who remember the quieter times with a sentimental attachment feel that this breakneck development is a change for the worse. For food, however, Bangkok has become one of the world's most interesting capitals. There is almost every kind of cuisine represented here, some to the highest international standards. At midday and in the evening, food seems to dominate Bangkok. It might not be true that there are more eating establishments per square kilometre here than anywhere else in the world, as has been claimed, but it certainly looks that way. Apart from the restaurants, every street corner has stalls selling noodles, fried chicken, sausages on sticks and countless other snacks. Some lanes are completely full of such stalls, wheeled in by their proprietors for the lunchtime or evening rush; pavements and sidewalks are crowded with tables and chairs.

Basically, Bangkok is a city where, like Paris, food is taken seriously. Well, perhaps serious is not quite the right word for the Thai approach to eating out, for Thais are among the least intense people in their daily lives. But food plays an important part, and Bangkok Thais are very discriminating in what and where they eat. Most people have strong opinions about the best places that serve their favourite dishes, and eating out is one of the most popular pastimes.

Not surprisingly, all the various regional cuisines are represented in the capital, although for some reason Northern food receives less attention than the others. Yet Bangkok has its own specialities and for these, as well

as its sheer exuberance and concentration of food-related activities, it deserves to be treated as a region in its own right.

The two distinctive cuisines of the capital are Palace cooking and Chinese. Royal, or Palace, cuisine represents the elegant side of Thai food. Most Thai dishes – and certainly all the most popular ones – are stronger on taste than on appearance, and the blending of flavours, while often subtle, is rarely delicate. Palace cooking in contrast offers exquisitely presented dishes and more refined tastes (though not necessarily superior). These are dishes created for the courts of different centuries; they were invented and adapted rather than evolved from easily available foodstuffs.

Where the Chaophaya River flows through Bangkok, its banks are a jumble of activity. Landing stages jut out everywhere; markets, business offices and houses back onto the water, and the river traffic of rice barges, ferries and narrow, noisy 'long-tail' boats never stops. A little way south of the Grand Palace, however, is the most jumbled, most frantic section of all, with a bustle of activity surprising even for this city. This is Chinatown, and, like Chinatowns everywhere in the world, is the hub of small-scale trading and commerce. From a culinary point of view it is also the epicentre of Thai-Chinese cooking. While the broad base of the food served here is Southern Chinese, the immigrants who have settled here from the city's earliest days have adapted their cuisine to accommodate local food ingredients, in particular local species of fish.

Many dishes in Bangkok which to the casual visitor seem to be perfectly Thai in character are often basically Chinese. Noodles – *kwitiaow* to the Thais – are so ubiquitous that it is easy to overlook the fact that they are a Chinese import, albeit a very ancient and successful one. Not even the name has changed: you can use the same word at a street stall in Hong Kong.

LEFT *Bangkok's Royal Palace and Temple complex, illuminated for the King's 60th birthday celebrations – the full moon is no coincidence.*

TOP RIGHT *Plaa khem (salt fish) and kung haeng (dried shrimps) in Bangkok's Chatuchak market.*

RIGHT *A lotus seller.*

KRATONG THONG

Golden baskets

A classy opening dish to a meal, these crisp, deep-fried batter cases can also be presented as a delicate snack. The only significant problem is to find a suitable metal mould; a tiny ladle might do, but the dimensions should be no more than a couple of inches/ 5 cm across. The Thai moulds are made from brass. You can make these cases in advance; sealed in a biscuit barrel or jar, they will keep for a long time.

• SERVES FOUR–SIX •

BATTER

½ cup/2 oz/50 g rice flour
6 tbsp plain (all-purpose) flour
4 tbsp thin coconut milk
2 tbsp tapioca flour
1 egg yolk
¼ tsp sugar
¼ tsp salt
¼ tsp baking soda (bicarbonate of soda)
approx. 4 cups/32 fl oz/900 ml peanut or corn oil for
deep-frying

FILLING

2 tbsp peanut or corn oil
4 tbsp finely diced onion
1 cup/6 oz/175 g finely chopped cooked pork or chicken
¼ cup/1½ oz/40 g sweetcorn (corn kernels)
2 tbsp finely diced raw potato
2 tbsp finely diced carrot
2 tbsp sugar
¼ tsp black soya sauce
½ tsp salt
½ tsp ground white pepper
coriander sprigs for garnish
1 fresh small red chilli, sliced finely into circles, for garnish

Mix all the batter ingredients together well in a bowl. Heat the oil in a pan or wok to about 180°F/350°C. Dip the kratong moulds in the oil to heat up, remove and pat lightly with kitchen paper (paper towel). Then dip the outside of the moulds into the batter and quickly into the hot oil again. Fry until light brown, about 5–8 minutes, remove the cups from the moulds and place on kitchen paper (paper towel) to dry. Repeat to make 20–25 cups.

Now make the filling. Put the 2 tbsp oil in a hot wok or pan, add the onion and pork, and stir-fry for 2 minutes. Add the rest of the ingredients and fry until the vegetables are fairly soft, about 3 minutes. Take off the heat and allow to cool. Divide the filling between the batter cups. Garnish with coriander leaves and small pieces of fresh red chilli.

Serve as an hors d'oeuvre or with cocktails.

KHAO PHAD KAI

Chicken fried rice

One of the basic standard Thai dishes, this always tastes best with rice from the day before – and is easier to cook if the rice has been chilled in the fridge for a while. In place of chicken, pork or prawns (shrimps) are also commonly used.

• SERVES FOUR •
3 tbsp peanut or corn oil
7 oz/200 g boneless skinned chicken breasts, cut lengthwise
into ½ in/1 cm thick slices
1 tbsp chopped garlic
1 medium-sized onion, sliced
2 eggs

4 cups/1¾ lb/750 g cooked rice
1 tomato, cut into 8 wedges
1 spring onion (scallion), chopped
2 tsp white soya sauce
1 tsp fish sauce
1 tsp sugar
1 tsp ground white pepper

Heat the oil in a wok or pan, add the chicken and garlic and mix well over the heat for 1 minute. Add the onion and cook for 1 minute, break in the eggs, mix very well and then stir in the rice and the rest of the ingredients. Stir well. Cook for 2 minutes and serve immediately.

Serve accompanied by cucumber slices, whole spring onions (scallions) and phrik nam plaa (page 25).

KHAO MAN KAI

Chicken rice

A very popular day-time dish, and Chinese in origin, khao man kai's special feature is that the rice is cooked in chicken broth (ideally, capon). The chicken pieces are always arranged on top of the mound of rice.

• SERVES FOUR •

11 oz/300 g boneless skinned capon or chicken breasts
5 cups/40 fl oz/1.25 ltr water
3 coriander roots
2 tsp salt
1 cup/8 oz/225 g rice, rinsed
10 garlic cloves, chopped
½ oz/15 g ginger, sliced and crushed
3 tbsp peanut or corn oil
5 in/12 cm piece of cucumber, cut into ¼ in/5mm slices
¼ cup/¼ oz/10 g coriander leaves
KHAO MAN SAUCE
5 fresh small green chillies, chopped
2 tbsp pickled soya beans
½ tbsp chopped ginger
½ tbsp white vinegar
1 tsp sugar
1 tsp black soya sauce
¼ tsp chopped garlic

Boil the water in a pan, add the chicken with the coriander root and salt, and cook until the chicken is soft, about 15 minutes. Remove the meat with a slotted spoon and put to one side. Strain the cooking liquid, put 4 cups/32 fl oz/900 ml back in the pan and add the rice, garlic, ginger and oil. Bring back to the boil and cook, covered, until the rice is tender but not soft, about 15-18 minutes.

Place the rice on serving plates. Slice the chicken across into ½ in/1 cm pieces and place on top of the hot rice. Arrange the cucumber slices around the sides and sprinkle with the coriander leaves.

Mix all the ingredients for the caw mon sauce together in a bowl and serve with the chicken and rice, and with the remaining cup of chicken broth if desired.

KWITIAOW RAAD NAA

Fried noodles with chicken, vegetables and gravy

If available, use the large flat noodles known as 'sen yai' (see page 15), rather than the thin variety.

• SERVES FOUR •

11 oz/300 g large flat rice noodles (sen yai)
½ cup/4 fl oz/100 ml peanut or corn oil
1 tsp black soya sauce
2 tbsp garlic, chopped finely
7 oz/200 g boneless skinned chicken breasts cut lengthwise into ½ in/1 cm thick slices
2 tbsp white soya sauce
2 tbsp sugar
1 tsp ground white pepper
6 cups/48 fl oz/1.35 ltr chicken stock
15 oz/400 g kale or broccoli, cut into ½ in/1 cm pieces
1 tbsp cornflour (cornstarch), mixed with a little water

Boil the noodles for 1 minute and drain well. Heat half the oil in a wok or pan, add the noodles and fry lightly for 1 minute. Add the black soya sauce, fry lightly for another minute. Drain off the oil and transfer the noodles to a plate.

Heat the rest of the oil in the wok. Add the garlic and chicken, and fry lightly for 2 minutes. Stir in the white soya sauce, sugar, white pepper and then the chicken stock. Boil well for 3–5 minutes, add the kale, boil again for 1 minute and then add the cornflour (cornstarch). Boil for 1 minute and pour over the noodles.

Serve accompanied by phrik dong (sliced fresh red chilli in vinegar), fish sauce, sugar and chilli powder, in separate bowls.

45

KAI PHAD MET MA MUANG

Chicken fried with cashew nuts

A delicious dish, of Chinese origin; very easy to make with impressive results.

• **SERVES FOUR** •

11 oz/300 g boneless skinned chicken breasts, cut into slices
plain (all-purpose) flour for coating
1 cup/8 fl oz/225 ml peanut or corn oil
4 dried red chillies, fried and cut into ½ in/1 cm pieces
1 tbsp chopped garlic
10 spring onions (scallions), white parts, cut into 2 in/5 cm pieces
⅓ cup/2 oz/50 g unsalted roasted cashew nuts
3 oz/75 g onion, sliced
2 tbsp oyster sauce
1 tbsp white soya sauce
1 tbsp sugar
⅛ tsp black soya sauce

Coat the chicken lightly with flour. Heat the oil in a pan or wok and fry the chicken for about 5 minutes until light brown. Remove almost all the oil from the pan.

Add the chilli and garlic to the chicken in the pan and fry for 1 minute. Add all the remaining ingredients; fry until cooked, about 3 more minutes.

Serve accompanied by rice.

PRIAW WAAN KAI

Sweet and sour chicken

A dish that is popular with most people. It is not spicy but a spoonful of fish sauce will add zest.

• **SERVES FOUR–SIX** •

4 cups/32 fl oz/900 ml peanut or corn oil
15 oz/400 g boneless skinned chicken breasts, cut across into ¼ in/5 mm slices
plain (all-purpose) flour for coating
1 medium-sized onion, sliced
1 medium-sized green pepper, sliced
½ cup/4 fl oz/100 ml tomato ketchup
½ cup/4 oz/100 g tomato quarters
½ cup/2 oz/50 g diced pineapple
½ cup/4 fl oz/100 ml chicken stock
2 tsp white soya sauce
1 tsp sugar
1 tsp white vinegar

Heat the oil in a wok or pan, coat the chicken lightly with flour and fry it until light brown, about 5 minutes. Remove and drain on kitchen paper (paper towel).

Remove all the oil except for about ⅓ cup/3 fl oz/75 ml. Add the onion and pepper, cook for 1 minute, mix in the ketchup, and then add the remaining ingredients. Stir-fry for 1 minute, add the chicken and continue to cook until the onion is tender, about 2 minutes.

Serve accompanied by rice and phrik nam plaa (page 25).

KAI PHAD PHRIK

Chicken fried with green pepper

• **SERVES FOUR** •

1/4 cup/2 fl oz/50 ml peanut or corn oil
1 tbsp chopped garlic
11 oz/300 g boneless skinned chicken breasts, cut lengthwise
into 1/2 in/1 cm thick slices
1 cup/5 oz/150 g sliced green pepper
5 fresh red chillies, sliced lengthwise
1/2 cup/3 oz/75 g thickly sliced onion
1 tbsp oyster sauce
1/2 tbsp white soya sauce
1 tsp fish sauce
1/4 tsp black soya sauce
1/2 cup/1/2 oz/15 g sweet basil leaves

Heat the oil in a wok or pan, add the garlic and chicken and
fry well for a minute. Add the green pepper and chilli, mix,
then add the onion and cook for 1 minute. One by one stir
in the rest of the ingredients, cooking for about 30 seconds
after each addition. Remove from the heat immediately after
stirring in the basil.

Serve accompanied by rice.

KAI PHAD KHING

Chicken fried with ginger

• SERVES FOUR •
⅓ cup/3 fl oz/75 ml peanut or corn oil
1 tbsp chopped garlic
11 oz/300 g boneless skinned chicken breasts, cut into ¼ in/
5 mm thick slices
1 oz/25 g wood fungus or fresh button mushrooms, sliced
4 spring onions (scallions), cut into 1 in/2.5 cm pieces
2 oz/50 g onion, sliced
1 oz/25 g ginger, cut into small matchsticks
3 fresh red chillies, each sliced into 6 strips lengthwise
1 tbsp white soya sauce
2 tsp brandy
½ tsp sugar
¼ tsp salt

Heat the oil in a wok or pan, add the garlic and stir-fry, mixing well. Add the chicken, mix well for 1 minute, and then add the mushrooms. Stir for a minute and add all the rest of the ingredients. Stir-fry well until the chicken is cooked, about 8–10 minutes.

Serve accompanied by rice and phrik nam plaa (page 25).

KAI PHAD KAPHRAO

Chicken fried with basil

• SERVES FOUR •
8 fresh green chillies, chopped lightly
8 garlic cloves, chopped lightly
¼ cup/2 fl oz/50 ml peanut or corn oil
11 oz/300 g boneless skinned minced (ground) chicken
2 fresh red chillies, quartered lengthwise
1 tbsp oyster sauce
½ tsp fish sauce
¼ tsp black soya sauce
⅓ cup/¾ oz/20 g sweet basil leaves

Pound the green chilli and garlic together with a mortar and pestle or in a blender. Heat the oil in a wok or pan until hot, then add the chilli-garlic mixture. Fry for 1 minute. Add the chicken and stir-fry for 1 minute; then add the red chilli, oyster sauce, fish sauce and soya sauce. Stir-fry for 2 minutes, mix the basil in well and serve immediately.

Serve accompanied by rice.

KHAO NAA PED

Duck with rice

A very popular dish, of Chinese origin, with two contrasting sauces.

• SERVES FOUR •

1 roasted duck (rub with red food colouring before roasting),
boned and cut into 2½ × ½ in/7 × 1 cm slices
4 cups/1¾ lb/750 g cooked rice
4 tbsp thinly sliced pickled ginger
4 tbsp thinly sliced sweet dill or pickled cucumber

COOKED SAUCE
2 cups/16 fl oz/450 ml chicken stock
1 tbsp sugar
½ tbsp white soya sauce
¼ tbsp black soya sauce
1 tsp flour

SOYA CHILLI RICE
½ cup/3 fl oz/75 ml black soya sauce
3 fresh red chillies, sliced thinly into circles
1 tbsp sugar
½ tbsp vinegar

Heat the ingredients for the cooked sauce together in a pan
and boil for 1 minute. Mix the ingredients for the raw sauce
in a bowl and put to one side.

Warm the duck and rice in a 350°F/180°C/gas 4 oven for 5
minutes. Then, divide the rice between 4 serving plates, and
arrange the duck meat over the top. Spoon the cooked sauce
on top of each, and place ginger and pickle slices around
the edges. Serve with the raw sauce on the side.

KAENG PED PED YANG

Red duck curry

This is a very popular dish in Thailand; rich and quite delicious.

• SERVES SIX •

7 cups/56 fl oz/1.55 ltr thin coconut milk
1 roasted duck, boned with skin left on, cut into ½ in/1 cm
slices
15 cherry tomatoes
5 fresh large red chillies, sliced lengthwise
1 cup/2½ oz/60 g sweet basil leaves
3 kaffir lime leaves, chopped

3 tbsp sugar
2 tbsp fish sauce
1 tsp salt

RED CURRY PASTE

3 stalks of lemon grass, sliced thinly
¼ cup/1½ oz/40 g chopped galangal (ka)
7 dried red chillies, chopped roughly
3 tbsp chopped garlic
1 tbsp shrimp paste
1 tsp chopped kaffir lime leaf
1 tsp chopped coriander root
1 tsp white peppercorns
½ tsp coriander seeds

Pound all the curry paste ingredients together with a mortar and pestle or in a blender to a fine paste.

Heat 2 cups/16 fl oz/450 ml of the coconut milk in a wok or pan, add the chilli paste mixture and cook together for 5 minutes. Add the rest of the coconut milk, bring to a boil, then add the duck, cherry tomatoes and red chilli. Bring back to the boil and then add the rest of the ingredients. Boil all together for 5 minutes and remove from the heat.

Serve accompanied by rice, salted eggs and sun-dried beef.

KHAO MOO DAENG

Red pork with rice

The red-coloured marinade soaks a little way into the meat from the surface; when sliced, the red edges of the pork make this a decorative as well as tasty dish.

• SERVES SIX •
11 oz /300 g pork loin
4 cups /32 fl oz /900 ml water
¼ cup /2 fl oz /50 ml tomato purée (paste)
3 tbsp white soya sauce
3 tbsp sugar
3 drops of red food colouring (optional)
1½ tbsp cornflour (cornstarch)
2 cups /12 oz /350 g cooked rice, heated
NAM CHIM SAUCE
4 tbsp white vinegar
2 tbsp black soya sauce
1 fresh red chilli, sliced thinly
¼ tsp sugar

Mix together the pork, water, tomato purée, soya sauce, sugar and food colouring in a bowl and leave to marinate for 1 hour.

Put the pork mixture with its marinade in a pan, bring to a boil and simmer for 30 minutes. Remove the pork and place in an ovenproof pan; roast it in a preheated 350°F/180°C/gas 4 oven for 10 minutes until lightly browned and glazed. Reserve the cooking liquid.

Mix a little of the cooking liquid with the cornflour (cornstarch) and then stir in 2 cups/16 fl oz/450 ml more liquid. Bring to a boil in a small pan to thicken, then remove from the heat.

Mix together the ingredients for the nam chim sauce. Slice the pork and place on serving plates (on top of the hot rice). Spoon the cornflour sauce over the top, and serve with the nam chim sauce on the side.

Serve accompanied by sliced cucumber, spring onions (scallions), hard-boiled eggs and pieces of deep-fried fresh pork fat back or pork belly.

MOO KRATHIAM PHRIK THAI

Pork fried with garlic and peppercorns

• SERVES FOUR–SIX •
approx. 3 cups /24 fl oz /675 ml peanut or corn oil for frying
11 oz /300 g pork loin, sliced into ¾ × 1 in /2 × 2.5 cm)
rectangles, ¼ in /5mm thick
2 tbsp chopped garlic
2 tsp black peppercorns, crushed lightly
1 tsp white soya sauce
1 tsp salt
¼ cup /¼ oz /10 g chopped coriander leaves
2 fresh red chillies, cut into lengthwise strips

Heat the oil in a wok or pan to 350°F/180°C. Fry the pork until light brown, about 8–10 minutes. Take out all but the meat and ½ cup/4 fl oz/100 ml of the oil, then add the garlic, peppercorns, soya sauce and salt. Stir-fry for 2 minutes or until the garlic is light brown.

Remove the pork mixture from the pan with a slotted spoon, drain well and place on a serving plate. Sprinkle with the coriander and chilli to garnish.

Serve accompanied by rice and sliced cucumber.

PLAA JIAN

Fried fish with pork and ginger

A relatively simple dish to prepare with any flat fish, plaa jian acquires considerable flavour from the pork fat, but is quite mild.

• SERVES FOUR •
11 oz/300 g whole pomfret fish, cleaned and gutted
½ tsp salt
½ cup/3 oz/75 g finely sliced pork belly or fresh fat back
2 salted preserved plums or 1 tbsp pickled lemon juice
¼ cup/1½ oz/40 g sliced ginger
10 small garlic cloves, crushed
½ cup/2 oz/50 g celery with its leaves, cut into 1 in/2.5 cm pieces
4 spring onions (scallions), cut into 1 in/2.5 cm pieces
2 fresh red chillies, cut into lengthwise strips

Wash and dry the fish and rub it inside and out with the salt. Place half the pork fat on a heatproof plate that fits a steamer, put the fish on top and cover with the rest of the pork fat. Roughly chop the salted plum and sprinkle it (or the juice) over the top together with the ginger and garlic.

Steam for 15 minutes, then add the celery, spring onion (scallion) and chilli and steam for 5 more minutes, until the fish is firm but tender.

Serve accompanied by rice.

YAM PLAA DUK FOO

Fried catfish spicy salad

In appearance and treatment, this is more an 'exploded' catfish salad. This crispy dish is often served as a snack to accompany drinks (an important and distinct category of dish in Thailand, where drinking tends to be separated from eating main meals).

• SERVES FOUR–SIX •
2 whole catfish (1 lb 2 oz/500 g each), cleaned and gutted
approx. 5 cups/40 fl oz/1.25 ltr peanut or corn oil for
deep-frying
1 green unripe mango, cut into matchsticks
1/4 cup/1 1/2 oz/40 g unsalted roasted peanuts
7 fresh small green chillies, chopped
3 tbsp sliced shallots
3 tbsp fish sauce
2 tbsp coriander leaves and stems cut into 1 in/2.5 cm pieces

Steam the catfish for 15 minutes until well cooked. Remove all the skin and bones and chop finely.

Heat the oil in a wok or pan until hot, about 350°F/180°C, sprinkle in the chopped fish and fry until light brown and crispy, 3–5 minutes. Remove with a slotted spoon or strainer and drain well.

Mix all the remaining ingredients except the coriander with the fish. Place the salad on plates, and garnish with coriander.

Serve accompanied by rice.

KUNG SOM

Prawn (shrimp) with lemon and coconut

The lemon, coconut and shrimp combination is wonderful. This is a good cocktail snack, too.

• SERVES FOUR–SIX •
1 lb 2 oz/500 g raw prawns (large shrimps), shelled
1 cup/8 fl oz/225 ml thin coconut milk
2 tbsp lemon juice
1/4 tsp fish sauce
1/4 tsp sugar
1/4 tsp salt
2 tbsp sliced shallots
5 fresh small green chillies, sliced into thin circles

To butterfly the prawns (shrimps), cut them lengthwise almost all the way through and splay them out.

Boil the coconut milk in a pan, add the prawns (shrimps), cook for 1 minute and remove the pan from the heat. Allow to stand for about 1 minute (until the prawns (shrimps) are just cooked), then remove them with a slotted spoon and place on a serving plate.

Add the lemon juice, fish sauce, sugar and salt to the coconut milk in the pan, stir well for 1 minute and then spoon this sauce over the prawns. Sprinkle over the shallot and chilli.

Serve accompanied by rice.

KUNG OP WOON SEN

Casseroled prawns (shrimps) with glass noodles

The size of the prawns is unimportant; you could use small shrimps or lobster tails. Another way of preparing this casserole is with crab claws.

• SERVES SIX •

2 bacon rashers, cut into 1 in/2.5 cm pieces
6 prawns (large shrimps), shelled
2 coriander roots, cut in half
1 oz/25 g ginger, pounded or chopped finely
1 oz/25 g garlic, chopped
1 tbsp white peppercorns, crushed
5 cups/1 lb/450 g cellophane noodles (woon sen), soaked in cold water for 10 minutes
1 tsp butter
3 tbsp black soya sauce
¼ cup/¼ oz/10 g roughly chopped coriander leaves and stems

SOUP STOCK
2 cups/16 fl oz/450 ml chicken stock
2 tbsp oyster sauce
2 tbsp black soya sauce
½ tbsp sesame seed oil
1 tsp brandy or whisky
½ tsp sugar

Place all the soup stock ingredients in a pan, bring to a boil and simmer for 5 minutes. Leave to cool.

Take a heatproof casserole dish or heavy-bottomed pan and place the bacon over the base. Put in the prawns (shrimps), coriander root, ginger, garlic and peppercorns. Place the noodles over the top, then add the butter, soya sauce and soup stock.

Place on the heat, cover, bring to a boil and simmer for 5 minutes. Mix well with tongs, add the coriander, cover and cook again until the prawns (shrimps) are cooked, about 5 minutes more. Remove excess stock liquid before serving.

neath. Place the sliced pork, liver and preserved cabbage on top of the noodles.

Boil the chicken stock in a pan, add the fish balls and boil for 3 minutes. Remove with a slotted spoon and add to the bowls.

Put the minced (ground) pork in a small pan with 1½ cups/ 12 fl oz/325 ml of the chicken stock and heat gently, mixing well until the pork is cooked, about 4–5 minutes. Add the spring onion (scallion), coriander, garlic and pepper, and then pour into the bowls. Top with more chicken stock as needed to fill each bowl.

Serve accompanied by fish sauce, chilli powder, sugar and phrik dong (sliced fresh red chillies in vinegar), all in separate bowls. Add these according to individual taste.

KWITIAOW NAM

Noodle soup

Very much a quick daytime dish, this soup is of Chinese origin but served all over Thailand – on the rivers and canals you can still see floating kwitiaow vendors in small, specially kitted-out boats. The ingredients vary from place to place, although fish balls are normally a constant. This version contains three varieties of pork.

• SERVES FOUR •
7 oz/200 g pork loin, cut into thin slices
15 oz/400 g thin rice vermicelli noodles (sen lek or sen mii)
3 cups/5 oz/150 g bean sprouts
4 oz/100 g pork liver, boiled and sliced thinly
1 tsp chopped preserved cabbage
8 cups/64 fl oz/1.8 ltr chicken stock
12 fish balls
½ cup/3 oz/75 g minced (ground) pork
1 spring onion (scallion), cut into ½ in/1 cm pieces
2 tbsp coriander leaves and stems, cut into ½ in/1 cm pieces
2 tbsp chopped garlic, fried in oil until golden
½ tsp ground white pepper

Boil the pork loin for about 15 minutes, cool slightly and cut into ½ in/1 cm thick strips. Set aside.

Cook the noodles and bean sprouts together lightly in boiling water for 3 minutes – don't cook until very soft. Drain and place in deep soup bowls, with the bean sprouts under-

MEE KROB

Sweet crisp-fried noodles

This is a Thai embellishment of a Chinese dish, and for complete success depends on the noodles being fried just right – so that they are both crisp and puffy when served.

• SERVES FOUR–SIX •
approx. 6 cups/48 fl oz/1.35 ltr peanut or corn oil for frying
7 oz/200 g raw medium-sized prawns (shrimps), shelled and cut into 3 pieces
5 oz/150 g pork loin, cut into cubes the same size as prawn pieces
½ cup/4 oz/100 g firm bean curd (tofu) cut into small rectangles
5 oz/150 g thin rice vermicelli noodles (sen mii), soaked in cool water for 1 minute if dried and drained well
½ tbsp chopped garlic
½ tbsp chopped onion
¼ cup/1½ oz/40 g palm sugar
2 tbsp white vinegar
1 tbsp marinated soya beans
1 tbsp fish sauce
3 cups/5 oz/150 g bean sprouts
3 spring onions (scallions), cut into 1½ in/4 cm pieces
2 tbsp sliced pickled garlic
2 fresh red chillies, cut into very thin strips

Heat the oil in a pan or wok and fry the prawns (shrimps) and pork until brown and well cooked, about 10 minutes. Remove with a slotted spoon and drain on kitchen paper (paper towel).

Add the bean curd (tofu) to the hot oil and fry until brown, about 2 minutes. Remove with a slotted spoon, and drain on kitchen paper (paper towel). Add the noodles to the hot oil and brown lightly, about 4–5 minutes. Remove and drain well.

Remove all the oil from the pan except for 2 tbsp. Add the garlic and onion and fry gently for a minute; then add the cooked pork, prawns (shrimps) and bean curd (tofu), the sugar, vinegar, marinated soya beans and fish sauce. Fry until thick and sticky, about 7–10 minutes.

Reduce the heat and add the noodles. Mix well for 1 minute, then transfer onto a large plate in a mound. Arrange the bean sprouts, spring onion (scallion), pickled garlic and chilli on top.

KHAO TOM KAI

Boiled rice soup with chicken

The traditional and universal Thai breakfast, tasty and nourishing. It is also made with minced (ground) pork, and an optional extra is an egg cracked straight into the dish just before serving; it partly poaches in the hot broth.

• SERVES FOUR •
6 cups/48 fl oz/1.35 ltr chicken stock
11 oz/300 g boneless skinned chicken breasts, cut across into thin slices
4 cups/1¾ lb/750 g cooked rice
1 tbsp chopped pickled cabbage
1 tsp salt
1 tsp ground white pepper
1 cup/4 oz/100 g finely sliced celery
2 spring onions (scallions), sliced
⅓ cup/2 oz/50 g garlic cloves, unpeeled and fried until soft
½ cup/3 oz/75 g phrik dong (sliced red chilli with vinegar)
2 tbsp fish sauce

Boil the chicken stock in a pan. Add the chicken, rice, cabbage, salt and pepper; boil the chicken until cooked, about 8–10 minutes. Add the celery and spring onion (scallion), and remove from the heat immediately.

Pour into bowls and sprinkle with the fried garlic. Serve with the phrik dong and fish sauce in separate bowls.

KHAO PHAD NAM PHRIK

Fried rice with spicy sauce

This is a spicier and more traditional version of the khao phad recipe on page 43. Nam phrik gives the dish flavour and nutritional value. A tasty lunchtime dish.

• SERVES FOUR–SIX •
2 tbsp peanut or corn oil
4 cups/1¾ lb/750 g cooked rice
3 tbsp phrik nam plaa sauce (see page 25)

Heat the oil in a wok or pan, add the rice and mix well, stir-frying for 1 minute. Add the sauce, mix well and cook for 1 more minute. Remove from the heat.

Serve accompanied by preserved salted eggs, cucumber slices, fried eggs and raw vegetables.

KHAO OP SAPPAROD

Pineapple rice

A 'show-off' dish that is quite easy to make but always impressive to present. Although the pineapple also adds flavour to the rice, there is scarcely any point attempting it just with pineapple pieces – appearance is everything.

• **S E R V E S   F O U R – S I X** •
1 pineapple
4 tbsp peanut or corn oil
3 cups/1¼ lb/550 g cooked rice
½ cup/3 oz/75 g finely diced ham
½ tbsp chopped garlic
¼ cup/2 oz/50 g raisins

2 tbsp chicken stock
2 tsp curry powder
1 tsp sugar
1 tsp salt
¼ tsp ground white pepper

Cut one side off the pineapple lengthwise to expose the inside. Carefully remove the inside fruit and cut into small dice. Reserve the outside of the pineapple.

Heat the oil in a pan or wok, add the ham and garlic, stir-fry, then add ½ cup/3 oz/75 g of the diced pineapple and all the rest of the ingredients. Mix well. Spoon into the empty pineapple, cover with the pineapple lid and bake in a preheated 275°F/140°C/gas 1 oven for 30 minutes.

YAM MAKHEUA YAO

Roasted aubergine (eggplant) salad

• SERVES SIX •

3 long green aubergines (eggplants), combined weight
approx 11 oz/300 g
⅛ cup/1 oz/25 g minced (ground) pork
3 tbsp peanut or corn oil
2 oz/50 g dried shrimps, rinsed in hot water and drained
2 oz/50 g shallots, sliced
5 fresh small green chillies, chopped roughly
2 tbsp lime juice

1 tsp fish sauce
¼ tsp sugar

Dry-roast the aubergines (eggplants) in a 350°F/180°C/gas 4 oven for about 15–20 minutes until soft, then cool, remove the skin and slice into 1 in/2.5 cm pieces.

Sauté the pork in a frying pan (skillet) or wok in a little oil over high heat until done, about 10 minutes. Mix the aubergine (eggplant), pork, shrimp and all the remaining ingredients together well in a bowl.

Serve accompanied by rice.

POPIA SOD

Fresh spring rolls

A bit time-consuming to prepare but with a good result; a nice change from oily, fried spring rolls.

• SERVES FOUR–SIX •

2 Chinese sweet sausages, combined weight approx.
4 oz/100 g
7 oz/200 g firm bean curd (tofu)
1 packed cup/7 oz/200 g crab meat
2 tbsp peanut or corn oil
2 eggs, beaten lightly
4 oz/100 g cucumber
8–12 spring roll wrappers (or crêpes; follow a standard recipe
and add 1 tbsp cornflour (cornstarch))
6 cups/11 oz/300 g bean sprouts, blanched lightly
7 oz/200 g spring onions (scallions)
SPRING ROLL SAUCE
1 cup/8 fl oz/225 ml chicken stock
1/3 cup/2 oz/50 g palm sugar
1/4 cup/2 fl oz/50 ml tamarind juice
1 tbsp cornflour (cornstarch)

Steam the Chinese sausages for about 8 minutes and then the bean curd (tofu) for about 3 minutes. Remove and cut both into long pieces about the width of a pencil and about 4 in/10 cm long. Steam the crab meat for 5 minutes and set aside.

Heat a non-stick shallow pan over medium heat, add a drop of oil and just enough egg to cover the bottom – it should resemble a thin pancake. Cook for a minute on each side. Make 8–12 thin omelettes in the same way. Roll them up and slice them into lengths the same size as the sausage and bean curd (tofu). Cut the cucumber and spring onions (scallions) into similar lengths too.

Take each spring roll wrapper or crêpe, lay it flat and place on 1 piece of bean curd (tofu), sausage, cucumber and spring onions (scallions). Add 1 tsp of crab, several strips of egg and some bean sprouts. Roll up carefully and cut each into 3 lengths.

Place all the sauce ingredients except the cornflour (cornstarch) in a pan, and boil for 5 minutes. Add the cornflour mixed with a drop of water, boil for 1 minute and take off the heat.

Serve cold or steamed for 1–2 minutes. Sprinkle with more crab to serve, a tsp of spring roll sauce and extra chopped spring onion (scallion) if liked. Serve the sauce alongside.

PHAK BUNG FAI DAENG

Stir-fried greens

Possibly the fastest dish to cook in Thailand, let alone anywhere else, phak bung fai daeng is properly made with the water plant variously known in English as morning glory, swamp cabbage, or water convolvulus. As this is a Chinese dish in origin, look for this in a Chinese supermarket – or else substitute spinach. In the up-country town of Phitsanulok, a few restaurants have developed a special way of serving it: the cook throws the stir-fried vegetables high into the air across the road to the opposite sidewalk, where the waiter deftly catches them on a plate . . . honestly, this really happens!

• SERVES FOUR–SIX •
3 tbsp peanut or corn oil
11 oz/300 g morning glory (swamp cabbage) leaves and
stems, cut into 4 in/10 cm lengths
¹/₂ cup/4 fl oz/100 ml chicken stock
2 tbsp marinated soya beans
1 tbsp chopped garlic

Heat the oil in a wok or pan until very hot. Add all the ingredients at once (watch for splattering), and stir-fry for about 2 minutes.

Serve accompanied by khao tom (page 57) or steamed rice.

PHAK PHAD RUAM MIT

Mixed stir-fried vegetables

• SERVES FOUR •

2½ oz/60 g mange-tout (snow peas)
2½ oz/60 g kale, sliced
2½ oz/60 g white cabbage, sliced
2½ oz/60 g broccoli florets and stems, sliced
2½ oz/60 g cauliflower florets
2½ oz/60 g asparagus, cut into 2 in/5 cm lengths
2½ oz/60 g Chinese or pak-choi cabbage, sliced
2½ oz/60 g button mushrooms, halved
2½ oz/60 g fresh baby corn, halved
½ cup/4 fl oz/100 ml chicken stock
½ tsp ground white pepper
¼ cup/2 fl oz/50 ml peanut or corn oil
3 tbsp finely chopped garlic

4 tbsp oyster sauce
1 tbsp white soya sauce
¼ tsp black soya sauce

Mix all the vegetables together in a bowl, pour over the stock and add the white pepper.

Heat a wok or pan until lightly smoking and add the oil. When hot, add the garlic and stir well. Add the vegetables and liquid all at once (watch for splashing), and stir-fry until almost cooked, about 3–4 minutes; the vegetables should still be slightly crisp.

Add the oyster sauce and soya sauces, mix well for 1 minute and serve.

Serve accompanied by rice; this dish goes well with most dishes.

KAI YAD SAI

Stuffed omelette

This is a rapidly made lunchtime dish, more easily available in
markets and roadside stalls than in restaurants.

• SERVES FOUR •
¼ cup/2 fl oz/50 ml peanut or corn oil
½ cup/3 oz/75 g minced (ground) pork
3 tbsp finely diced tomatoes
3 tbsp peas
2 tbsp finely diced green pepper
2 tbsp finely diced onion
½ tbsp sugar
1 tsp fish sauce
¼ tsp ground white pepper
¼ tsp black soya sauce
3 eggs, beaten
3 tbsp coriander leaves for garnish
finely sliced red chilli for garnish

Heat half of the oil in a pan or wok over high heat and fry
the pork lightly for about 2 minutes. Add all the remaining
ingredients except for the eggs and rest of oil. Fry until fairly
thick, about 5–8 minutes, then set aside.

Heat a shallow non-stick or good omelette pan, add a drop
of the remaining oil and pour in enough egg to thinly cover
the base. Brown the omelette lightly on both sides, flipping
over half-way through cooking. Place a spoon of pork mixture in the centre, fold 2 opposite sides toward the centre
and then fold in the remaining 2 sides so that it resembles
a square.

Flip onto a serving plate and repeat until all the egg and
pork mixture is used up. Garnish with coriander leaves and
finely sliced red chilli.

Serve accompanied by rice.

LOOK CHOOP

Imitation fruits

This refined dessert was invented for the court and originally was served only at the Royal Palace. Even today it is hardly common, because of the time and skill needed to fashion these perfect miniatures of fruits and vegetables. They are spectacular to serve to guests, but only attempt them on a day when you have plenty of time to spare!

• SERVES SIX–EIGHT •
2 cups/12 oz/350 g dried mung beans
2 cups/16 fl oz/450 ml water
1 cup/8 fl oz/225 ml thin coconut milk
1 cup/6 oz/175 g + 1 tbsp sugar
edible food colourings
1 cup/8 fl oz/225 ml water
2 tbsp agar agar or gelatine

Place the mung beans in a container with the water and steam until soft, about 15 minutes, then pound them into a fine paste with a mortar and pestle or in a blender. Put in a pan with the coconut milk and 1 cup of the sugar, and heat slowly, stirring constantly, until very thick – about 15 minutes. Remove and allow to cool.

When cool, shape the paste into small fingertip-sized fruit and vegetable shapes – oranges, bananas – it's up to your imagination. Stick them on toothpicks and stand them in a sheet of polystyrene or styrofoam. Using a small paint brush and food colourings in appropriate shades, paint the fruits.

Heat the water, 1 tbsp of the sugar and the agar agar in a pan until dissolved. Cool slightly and then dip in the painted fruits. Place them back on the foam and allow to dry for 15 minutes; then dip once more in the liquid, spinning the fruit slowly after removing them so that the syrup coats evenly. Leave to harden on the foam, then remove the toothpicks and decorate the fruits with any (non-poisonous) leaves of your choice, trimmed down to a small size.

Serve as a special dessert.

THE SOUTH

South of Bangkok, the country rapidly narrows to a strip of land little more than 40 miles (25 km) wide in places. With the gulf of Thailand on one side, and Burma and the Andaman Sea on the other, this neck of territory is the Isthmus of Kra, connecting Thailand with the Malay Peninsula.

The connection is more than just geographical. While for most Westerners Thailand is synonymous with Buddhist temples, the cultural landscape of the South comes as something of a surprise – it is distinctly Malay and Muslim. South of the country's two main tourist resorts – Phuket Island on the west coast and Hat Yai on the east – Thailand borders Malaysia, and the cuisine is heavily influenced by Malay preferences.

The Malays in their turn have absorbed a considerable amount of Arabic culture. Mosques and the chant of the muezzin drifting across towns and villages calling the faithful to prayer are the first and most obvious signs to the visitor, but some of the dishes too are reminders of the Middle East and Pakistan: roti, *kaeng kari* and mussulman curry, spiced and prepared in an almost North Indian manner.

As in the upper part of the Gulf, the sea dominates the traditional livelihood of the South, and provides the main part of the diet. Here, though, there are two seas to fish, with slightly different catches. Coconut palms also give the landscape of the South much of its character, in favoured places backing long white sand beaches. They are the basis of a thriving and important copra industry and, not surprisingly, feature in a number of dishes. Southern cooking does not conspicuously use fewer chillies than the rest of Thailand, but the thickening of the coconut milk softens some of the fire.

LEFT *A view from Phuket.*

RIGHT *Hauling the nets at Koh Samui.*

BELOW *A fishing boat at rest after a night at sea.*

KAENG KARII KAI

Yellow chicken curry

An Indian-influenced curry dish very popular in Thailand.

• SERVES SIX •
5 cups/40 fl oz/1.25 ltr thin coconut milk
1 lb/450 g chicken, cut into medium-sized pieces
7 oz/200 g potatoes, peeled and cut into ½ in/1 cm cubes
2 tsp salt
3 tbsp sliced shallots, fried until light brown
YELLOW CURRY PASTE
5 dried red chillies, chopped
10 small garlic cloves, chopped
½ stalk of lemon grass, sliced
½ tbsp sliced shallot
2 tsp curry powder
1 tsp sliced ginger
1 tsp sliced galangal (ka)
1 tsp shrimp paste
1 tsp salt
½ tsp coriander seeds
½ tsp fennel seeds

Pound all the curry paste ingredients together with a pestle and mortar or in a blender to form a fine paste.

Heat 1 cup/8 fl oz/225 ml of the coconut milk in a wok or pan and cook the curry paste for 5 minutes. Add the rest of the coconut milk, bring to a boil, add the chicken and cook until tender, about 10 minutes. Add the potato and salt, and cook until the potatoes are done, about 10 minutes. Pour into soup bowls and sprinkle with the fried shallots.

Serve accompanied by ajaad salad (page 73), sliced pickled ginger and rice.

PANAENG NEUA

Coconut beef curry

This is one of the driest of Thai curries, and usually quite fiery.

• SERVES EIGHT •
¼ cup/2 fl oz/50 ml peanut or corn oil
11 oz/300 g beef sirloin, cut into 1¼ × ¾ × ¼ in/
3 × 2 × 1 cm pieces
3 cups/24 fl oz/675 ml thin coconut milk
1 tbsp fish sauce
2 tsp sugar
2 fresh red chillies, sliced
2 kaffir lime leaves, sliced finely
⅓ cup/¾ oz/20 g sweet basil leaves
CURRY PASTE
6 dried red chillies, chopped roughly
7 white peppercorns
1½ oz/40 g garlic, chopped roughly
1 oz/25 g shallots, chopped roughly
2 coriander roots, chopped roughly
2 tsp salt
1 tsp roughly chopped galangal (ka)
1 tsp roughly chopped lemon grass
1 tsp roughly chopped kaffir lime zest
1 tsp shrimp paste

Pound all the curry paste ingredients together with a mortar and pestle or in a blender to form a paste.

Heat the oil in a pan or wok and fry the curry paste for 3–4 minutes. Add the beef and fry for 2 minutes, then add the coconut milk and boil until the beef is tender, about 15 minutes. Add the fish sauce, sugar and chilli. Remove from the heat, transfer to a serving plate and sprinkle with the lime zest and basil.

Serve accompanied by rice.

KAENG MUSSAMAN

Muslim curry

Originally from India, as the cardamom, cloves and cinnamon suggest, and then tailored to Thai tastes, this curry can be made with either chicken or beef, but never pork.

• SERVES SIX •

5 cardamom seeds
1 cinnamon stick
6 cups/48 fl oz/1.35 ltr thin coconut milk
1 lb 2 oz/500 g beef (sirloin or stewing) or chicken, cut into
¾ in/2 cm cubes
7 oz/200 g potatoes, peeled and cut into ¾ in/2 cm cubes
1½ oz/40 g unsalted peanuts
10 shallots
3 bay leaves
3 tbsp palm sugar
3 tbsp fish sauce
3 tbsp tamarind sauce

CHILLI PASTE

2 oz/50 g shallots, chopped
10 small garlic cloves, chopped roughly
6 dried red chillies, seeded and chopped roughly
5 white peppercorns
1 tbsp chopped lemon grass
1 tsp salt
1 tsp chopped galangal (ka)
1 tsp fennel seeds
1 tsp shrimp paste
½ tsp cloves

Mix all the ingredients for the chilli paste together and fry in a dry pan until fragrant. Then pound them with a mortar and pestle or process in a blender until fine. Put to one side.

Dry-fry the cardamom seeds and cinnamon stick or dry-roast in a 350°F/180°C/gas 4 oven, for 8 minutes until fragrant.

Heat the chilli paste with 2 cups/16 fl oz/450 ml of the coconut milk in a wok or pan for about 5 minutes. Add the beef and fry until cooked, about 8–10 minutes. Add the rest of the coconut milk, bring to a boil and simmer lightly for 10 minutes. Add all the remaining ingredients and cook until the potatoes and meat are tender, about 15 minutes.

Serve accompanied by sliced pickled ginger, pickled vegetables and rice.

KAENG SOM

Sour curry soup

A delicious soup with lots of vegetables. The bones are cooked with the fish for more flavour.

• SERVES FOUR •

15 oz/400 g whole freshwater fish, cleaned and gutted
5 cups/40 fl oz/1.25 ltr water
2 oz/50 g cucumber, quartered and sliced lengthwise
2 oz/50 g green (string) beans, cut into 2 in/5 cm pieces
2 oz/50 g morning glory (swamp cabbage), cut into 2 in/
5 cm pieces
2 oz/50 g Chinese or pak choi cabbage, cut into 2 in/5 cm
pieces
3 tbsp tamarind juice
2 tbsp fish sauce
2 tsp lemon juice
1 tsp palm sugar

CHILLI PASTE
8 dried red chillies, chopped
2 oz/50 g shallots, chopped
1 tbsp chopped krachai
1 tbsp salt
½ tsp shrimp paste

Cut the fish into 1½ in/4 cm long pieces. Boil 5 oz/150 g of it in water until cooked, then remove with a slotted spoon (discard the water) and allow to cool. Remove all the bones, but retain the skin.

Pound all the chilli paste ingredients together well with a mortar and pestle or in a blender. Mix in the cooked fish pieces and pound or process again.

Place the fish-chilli paste in a pan or wok large enough to hold all the ingredients, add the 5 cups/40 fl oz/1.25 ltr water and bring to a boil. Add the rest of the fish, boil again for 2 minutes, then add the cucumber, beans, morning glory and cabbage. Bring back to a boil, add the rest of the ingredients and simmer for 10 minutes.

Serve accompanied by rice, sun-dried beef or dry salted fish, and pickled vegetables as condiments.

KAENG PHRIK

Southern chilli curry

As with most of the nam phriks, this thick, spicy southern curry is intended to be eaten with plain rice. Don't be fooled by the simplicity: it's both tasty and satisfying.

• SERVES FOUR •
2½ cups/20 fl oz/550 ml water
8 oz/225 g pork loin, cut into 1¼ × ¾ × ¼ in/
3 × 2 × ½ cm pieces
3 tbsp fish sauce
1 tsp curry powder
3 kaffir lime leaves, torn into quarters
CHILLI PASTE
8–10 g dried small green and red chillies, chopped
6 white peppercorns
2 tbsp sliced shallot
1 tbsp sliced garlic
1 tsp sliced galangal (ka)
1 tsp shrimp paste
¼ stalk of lemon grass, sliced

Pound all the ingredients for the chilli paste finely with a mortar and pestle or in a blender.

Boil the water in a pan or wok, add the chilli paste and boil briefly before adding the pork, fish sauce, curry powder and lime leaf. Boil again for 10 minutes before transferring to bowls.

Serve accompanied by rice.

NAM PHRIK JON

Southern vegetable dip

• SERVES FOUR •
½ cup/3 oz/75 g raw prawns (large shrimps), shelled and cut into 3 pieces
2 tbsp fish sauce
2 tbsp lemon or lime juice
1 tbsp chopped fresh small green chilli
1 tbsp sliced shallot
1½ tsp shrimp paste

Boil the prawns (shrimps) in a small amount of water for 2 minutes and drain. Place in a bowl and mix well with the rest of the ingredients except the shrimp paste.

Wrap the shrimp paste in foil, and roast in a 350°F/180°C/gas 4 oven for 5 minutes, or dry-fry in a hot wok for 3 minutes.

Remove and stir into the prawn mixture.

Serve accompanied by green (string) beans, butter (lima) beans, raw cabbage and rice.

KHAO YAM

Rice salad

This is another 'leftover' dish made with rice from a previous occasion – the southern version.

• SERVES FOUR–SIX •
2 cups/12 oz/350 g cooked rice
2 cups/8 oz/225 g unsweetened grated coconut, browned in a 350°F/180°C/gas 4 oven for 5–8 minutes
1 small pomelo or grapefruit, shredded
½ cup/2 oz/50 g dried shrimps, chopped
½ cup/1 oz/25 g bean sprouts
½ cup/3 oz/75 g finely sliced lemon grass
¼ cup/1½ oz/40 g sliced green (string) beans
2 dried red chillies, pounded
1 tbsp finely shredded kaffir lime leaf
SAUCE
1 cup/8 fl oz/225 ml water
2 tbsp chopped anchovies
1 tbsp palm sugar
2 kaffir lime leaves, torn into small pieces
¼ tsp sliced lemon grass

Put all the sauce ingredients in a pan, boil for 5 minutes, remove from the heat and strain. Put to one side.

Place the rice in half-cup moulds or large ramekins, press and invert onto a large serving platter. Arrange the rest of the raw ingredients around the edge of the rice in separate piles. To eat, spoon some rice onto individual plates and take a little of each ingredient to mix with the rice according to taste. Spoon the sauce over the top.

PHAD SATOR

Fried flat beans with pork

As I suggest in the recipe, you can use fresh butter (lima) beans as a substitute for the sator beans, but really the basis for this quintessentially southern dish is the strange flavour of the latter. The recipe is included here for authenticity and just in case you are able to find the real sator beans in a Thai delicatessen or greengrocer.

• SERVES FOUR •

3 fresh yellow or green chillies, chopped
1 tbsp chopped garlic
½ tsp shrimp paste
2 tbsp peanut or corn oil
5 oz/150 g pork loin (or chicken, or prawns/shrimps), cut into thin strips
2 cups/12 oz/350 g fresh sator or butter (lima) beans
½ tsp fish sauce
½ tsp sugar
½ tsp lime or lemon juice

Pound the chillies and garlic together with a pestle and mortar or in a blender to a fine paste. Mix with the shrimp paste.

Heat the oil in a pan or wok. Add the chilli-garlic mixture, then add the pork and stir-fry for 3 minutes. Add the beans and all the remaining ingredients, plus 3 tbsp water if using butter (lima) beans, then fry until the beans are cooked, about 10 minutes – they should be quite firm.

Serve accompanied by rice.

MOO SATEI

Pork satei

Now popular all over Thailand, and a speciality of market food stalls, satei arrived in the south from Indonesia, via Malaysia. Satei can be made with pork, chicken or beef; serve all together for variety.

• SERVES FOUR–SIX •

1 lb/450 g pork loin, cut into 3 × ¾ × ¼ in/
7.5 × 2 × ½ cm long slices
1½ cups/12 fl oz/325 ml thin coconut milk
5 kaffir lime leaves, chopped roughly
5 coriander roots, crushed
2 stalks of lemon grass, chopped roughly
1 tbsp curry powder
1 tsp palm sugar
½ tsp salt
SATEI SAUCE
⅓ cup/2 oz/50 g dried yellow mung beans
5 cups/40 fl oz/1.25 ltr thin coconut milk
1 cup/5 oz/150 g unsalted roasted peanuts, chopped very finely
4 oz/100 g chilli paste (see kaeng mussaman, page 69)
2 oz/50 g chilli paste (see kaeng ped ped yang, page 50)
3 tbsp palm sugar
2 tsp tamarind juice
1 tsp salt

AJAAD SALAD
2 cups/16 fl oz/450 ml white vinegar
1/3 cup/2 oz/50 g sugar
1 tsp salt
1 small (5 in/12 cm) cucumber, quartered and sliced lengthwise
1/4 cup/1 1/2 oz/40 g sliced shallots
2 fresh red chillies, sliced thinly into circles

Mix the pork with all the other ingredients in a bowl and leave to marinate for 3–4 hours. Then skewer the meat onto wood or metal skewers and grill (broil), preferably over charcoal.

While the pork is marinating, soak the mung beans in water for 1 hour, then drain and steam them for 20 minutes or until soft. Mash or purée in a food processor.

Next, make the satei sauce. Mix all the ingredients together and boil in a pan or wok for 5 minutes. Remove from the heat and leave to cool.

To make the ajaad salad, boil the vinegar, sugar and salt together in a pan until reduced to about 1 cup/8 fl oz/ 225 ml, take off the heat, cool and mix with the cucumber, shallots and chillies.

Serve the kebabs (kabobs) with the satei sauce and ajaad salad, with pieces of toasted bread to dip into the sauce.

ROTI
Southern flat breads

These are derived from Thailand's Indian connections, as the name suggests. Bread is uncharacteristic of Thai cooking, and roti are used mainly in this way, as a dessert snack.

• **MAKES SEVEN–EIGHT** •
approx. 1 1/2 cups/6 oz/175 g plain (all-purpose) flour
1/4 cup/2 fl oz/50 ml water
1 tbsp butter, softened
1 egg
1/4 tsp salt
1 cup/8 fl oz/225 ml approx. peanut or corn oil for frying

Mix all the ingredients except the oil together well in a bowl; if the mixture is too wet to shape, add a little more flour. Shape the dough into lime-sized balls and flatten them; flatten them into 4 in/10 cm circles by throwing them onto a lightly floured table surface – be careful to throw them quite horizontal.

Heat enough oil to just cover the bottom of a frying pan over medium heat. Place the flattened dough balls in the pan and brown lightly, about 3–4 minutes, on each side. Drain on kitchen paper (paper towel) and repeat.

Three delicious ways of serving roti are: to place an egg on top of each browned roti, flipping it over to cook the egg and rolling it up to eat (perhaps with coffee!); to sprinkle them with sugar and condensed milk; or to spread them with butter.

THE NORTH

Nowadays, most travellers to the North fly directly to Chiangmai, less than an hour from the capital by air. The more traditional, and to my mind the more pleasant and relaxing journey, is still however by rail. From Hua Lampong station in Bangkok the train clatters out of the city in the early evening, on through the night past Ayutthaya, Nakhon Sawan and Phitsanu-lok, taking a full fourteen hours to reach the Northern capital (Thai railways are noted for running at a leisurely pace).

The gentle gradients of the journey belie the fact that, until the early years of this century, Northern Thailand was effectively isolated from the rest of the country. Cut off by dense forests and the rapids of the Ping River, the North remained a quasi-independent kingdom and principality until Bangkok began to rule directly in 1877. The first convenient route to Chiangmai was the railway, not built until 1921.

King Mengrai, who established his kingdom of Lanna, as the seven Northern provinces are still called, was a contemporary of King Ram-kamhaeng, the founder of Siam. Not surprisingly, the North still retains a sense of cultural identity that sets it slightly apart from the rest of the country. This is a land of cool winters, hilly ranges separating small fertile valleys, pale-skinned and more Chinese-looking people who speak a distinct regional dialect, and of course a very particular regional cusine.

Unfortunately for many foreign visitors, their first, and often only, ex-perience of Northern Thai food is the heavily promoted 'Khan Toke' din-ners, a tourist industry creation that has about as much to with real North-ern cooking as does an airport gift shop with indigenous crafts. Northern food is robust, full of sharp country flavours, and by no means sophisti-cated. This is the antithesis of the downtown Bangkok restaurant serving elegant dishes in the Royal manner – and much the better for it.

A number of things set the Northern cuisine apart. Far north of the Gulf of Thailand, there are no naturally occurring coconut palms, and coconut milk plays an insignificant part; the curries are clear and spicy rather than milky and thickened. The traditional staple is *khao niaow*, sticky rice, eaten by kneading it into a small pad to use as a scoop for the dips and chopped meats that make up an important part of this region's dishes. Interestingly, sticky rice (which is quite firm and dry when properly cooked, and not at all gooey) was almost certainly the staple of the original Tai immigrants

who first settled here in large numbers in the thirteenth century, moving south from what is now Yunnan and Laos. Contemporary accounts support the idea that the Tai brought with them the eating habits of Southwest China. Marco Polo, in Yunnan in the thirteenth century, wrote of the custom of eating what sounds like the original version of steak tartare: 'They chop it [the meat] up small, put it in garlic sauce, and eat it there and then.' And indeed, a spiced preparation of finely chopped meat known as *laab*, tradi-tionally eaten raw and flavoured with a dash of bile, is still one of the North's famous dishes.

Bile may sound a strange ingredient to a Westerner – possibly even repugnant – but a hint of bitterness from one source or another is a theme that runs through a number of Northern Thai dishes, and is often provided by an astonishing variety of leaves culled from field and forest plants. True Northern food is found in the villages, and the liberal use of uncultivated herbs and other plants is very characteristic. It also makes a number of the dishes difficult to reproduce authentically. Fresh, raw vegetables are an essential feature of a Northern dinner table, and the more interesting flavours you can assemble, the better. Even if it means adding herbs and leaves that are alien to Thailand, I believe you can get more of the spirit of this regional cuisine by picking home-grown plants – easy enough to do

OPPOSITE PAGE
Threshing rice.

LEFT *Before the rice is planted, festivals are held to pray for plentiful rain for a good harvest.*

RIGHT *The lush green fields which mean food for people throughout and even outside the country.*

even in a small garden. Arugula or roquette, for instance, has a sharp flavour that seems to me a good substitute garnishing for, say, a Northern Thai *laab*. At all costs avoid the bland vegetables that nowadays grace most supermarket shelves. In much the same way that Northern villagers enjoy adding wild plants to their food, there is also a preference here for using offal: intestines, heart, liver, tongue, stomach and so on. To what extent you include these in your own versions of Northern meat dishes is a matter of personal preference. They undoubtedly add flavour – and texture of a kind – but are not to everyone's taste.

Traditionally, fish play a less important part in the diet here than in any of Thailand's other regions: in this hilly country, most of the rivers are relatively fast and narrow, and there are few natural lakes. More recently, of course, fish farms have been successful, but the original country menus are composed mainly of meat and vegetable dishes, and in particular of the distinct Northern versions of *nam phrik,* the characteristic Thai spicy dips.

MIENG KUM

Thai hors d'oeuvre

A hard-to-find treat in Thailand, but always enjoyed. The Thais use fresh tree and vine leaves, but I substitute lettuce. A dish well worth the trouble to prepare.

• SERVES SIX–EIGHT •

5 tbsp unsweetened grated coconut, roasted in a 350°F/ 180°C/gas 4 oven until light brown
3 tbsp finely diced shallots
3 tbsp finely diced lime
3 tbsp diced ginger
3 tbsp chopped dried shrimps
3 tbsp unsalted roasted peanuts
2 tsp chopped fresh small green chillies
1 lettuce or bunch of edible vegetable leaves

SAUCE

2 tbsp unsweetened grated coconut
½ tbsp shrimp paste
½ tsp sliced galangal (ka)
½ tsp sliced shallot
3 tbsp chopped unsalted peanuts
2 tbsp chopped dried shrimps
1 tsp sliced ginger
1 cup/6 oz/175 g palm sugar
2½ cups/20 fl oz/550 ml water

First, make the sauce: roast the shrimp paste, galangal and shallot in an 350°F/180°C oven for 5 minutes until fragrant, and cool. Place with the peanuts, shrimps and ginger in a blender or food processor and finely chop, or pound with a mortar and pestle until fine.

Transfer the mixture into a heavy-bottomed pan with the sugar and water, mix well and bring to a boil; simmer until it is reduced to about 1¼ cups/10 fl oz/275 ml. Remove from the heat and leave to cool.

To serve, pour the sauce into a serving bowl and arrange all the ingredients in separate piles on a platter or in small bowls. To eat, take a lettuce leaf, place a small amount of each of the garnishes in the middle, top with a spoonful of sauce and fold up into a little package.

KAENG HO

Northern mixed curry

A dish that is usually made with leftovers: here I use two different dishes with a few extras.

• S E R V E S   S I X •

3 tbsp peanut or corn oil
1 quantity chilli paste (see kaeng liang, page 79)
½ recipe kaeng ok kai, strained (see below)
½ recipe kaeng heng yod, strained (see page 79)
1 cup/4 oz/100 g cellophane noodles (woon sen), soaked in water for 5 minutes
¼ cup/2½ oz/60 g bamboo shoots
4 small white aubergines (eggplants), quartered
2 fresh red chillies, quartered lengthwise
lime or lemon juice, to taste
sugar, to taste

Heat the oil in a pan or wok, add the chilli paste and fry for 15 minutes. Add both cups of kaeng and stir-fry for 10 minutes, then add all the rest of the ingredients. Mix well, cook for another 10 minutes, and taste – it should be slightly sweet and sour; add lemon juice or sugar as necessary.

Serve accompanied by rice.

KAENG OK KAI

Northern chicken curry

A spicy chicken curry with no curry powder – chopped red chillies add the fire to this dish.

• S E R V E S   F O U R – S I X •

¼ cup/2 fl oz/50 ml peanut or corn oil
1 lb/450 g chicken (with skin and bone), cut into small pieces through the bones
6 cups/48 fl oz/1.35 ltr water
4 kaffir lime leaves, quartered
2 stalks of lemon grass, halved
1 tbsp fish sauce
CHILLI PASTE
10 dried red chillies, chopped roughly
2 tbsp finely sliced lemon grass
2 tbsp sliced shallots
½ tbsp sliced garlic
1 tsp galangal (ka)
1 tsp chopped coriander leaf
1 tsp shrimp paste
¼ tsp turmeric

Pound all the chilli paste ingredients to a fine paste with a mortar and pestle or in a blender.

Heat the oil in a pan, add the chilli paste and fry over medium heat for 1 minute. Add the chicken pieces, fry, then add the water and all the rest of the ingredients. Boil until the chicken is tender and the curry reduced to about half its original volume, about 20 minutes.

Serve accompanied by rice.

KAENG PHAKKAD CHO

Northern pork and spinach curry soup

• S E R V E S   F O U R – S I X •

3 cups/24 fl oz/675 ml water
1 lb/450 g pork spare ribs, cut into 1¼ in/3 cm pieces
½ tbsp tamarind juice
½ tbsp fish sauce
2 tsp chopped anchovies or dried salted fish
11 oz/300 g fresh spinach leaves
2 tsp sliced garlic
2 tsp sliced shallot
2 tbsp peanut or corn oil
4 whole dried red chillies

Boil the water in a pan, add the pork and bring back to a boil. Cook until the pork is tender, about 20–25 minutes. Add the tamarind juice, fish sauce and anchovy. Bring back to the boil, simmer for 5 minutes, add the spinach and remove from the heat after 1 minute. Transfer to a bowl.

Fry the garlic, shallot and chillies in the oil in a frying pan until tan-coloured. Sprinkle over the soup with the oil.

Serve accompanied by rice.

KAENG HANG LEI

Northern pork curry

A dish that originally comes from across the Burmese border, as shown by the use of tamarind and turmeric. The palm sugar adds an intentional slight sweetness.

• SERVES SIX •

4 stalks lemon grass, chopped
1 tbsp chopped galangal (ka)
1 tbsp shrimp paste
4 dried red chillies, chopped
2¼ lb/1 kg pork belly, cut into small ½ in/1 cm thick strips
3 cups/24 fl oz/675 ml cold water
1 tbsp turmeric
1 tsp black soya sauce
10 shallots, sliced

¼ cup/1½ oz/40 g palm sugar
¼ cup/1½ oz/40 g chopped and pounded ginger
¼ cup/2 fl oz/50 ml tamarind juice
2 tbsp chopped garlic
½ tbsp marinated soya beans
fish sauce, to taste (optional)

Pound the lemon grass, galangal, shrimp paste and chillies with a mortar and pestle or in a blender until fine, then mix with the pork. Put in a pan with the water, turmeric and soya sauce. Bring to a boil and cook until tender, about 15 minutes, then add the rest of the ingredients. Boil again for 5–8 minutes and remove from the heat. Taste and season with fish sauce if necessary.

KAENG HENG YOD

Northern Thai soup

• SERVES FOUR–SIX •
4 cups/32 fl oz/900 ml water
6 oz/175 g boneless skinned chicken breasts
1½ cups/10 oz/300 g minced (ground) pork
1 tbsp preserved cabbage
½ cup/3 oz/75 g sliced onion
2 tbsp fish sauce
½ oz/15 g dried large shrimps, soaked in cold water for 5 minutes
½ oz/15 g spinach leaf
2 tbsp tamarind juice

Boil the water in a pan, add the chicken and cook for 7–10 minutes until well cooked. Remove and cut across into thin slices. Using the same cooking water, add the pork, preserved cabbage, onion and fish sauce. Boil and then add the rest of the ingredients. Boil again before pouring into bowls.

Serve accompanied by rice.

KAENG LIANG

Spicy vegetable soup with prawns (shrimps)

• SERVES FOUR–SIX •
8 cups/64 fl oz/1.8 ltr chicken stock
7 oz/200 g pumpkin flesh, diced
5 oz/150 g banana flower, if available
4 oz/100 g young butternut squash, cut into wedges (with seeds)
4 oz/100 g green (string) beans, cut into 1 in/2.5 cm pieces
½ tbsp fish sauce
7 oz/200 g raw prawns (large shrimps), shelled
1 cup/2½ oz/60 g lemon basil leaves
CHILLI PASTE
4 oz/100 g shallots, sliced
10 white peppercorns
¼ cup/1 oz/25 g dried shrimps, chopped
3 fresh small green chillies, chopped
½ tbsp shrimp paste

Pound the chilli paste ingredients together with a mortar and pestle or in a blender.

Place the stock in a pan, add the chilli paste and bring to a boil. Add the vegetables, and boil for 10 minutes. Add the fish sauce, then add the prawn (shrimp) and lemon basil.
Cook for 3–5 minutes.

Serve accompanied by rice.

TOM HANG WUA

Oxtail soup

A North-eastern Thai version of a European and American favourite.

• SERVES FOUR–SIX •
1 lb/450 g oxtail, cleaned
7 cups/56 fl oz/1.55 ltr chicken stock
2 tsp white soya sauce
1 tsp salt
¼ tsp black peppercorns, crushed
3 coriander roots, crushed lightly
7 oz/200 g large potatoes, peeled and diced
7 oz/200 g tomatoes, quartered
10 fresh small green chillies, crushed and cut into 3
4 oz/100 g onions, cut into 6 pieces
1 tsp crushed garlic
¼ tsp sugar
2 tbsp chopped coriander leaves

Dry-roast in a 350°F/180°C/gas 4 oven or pan-fry the oxtail until brown. Remove the skin by scraping with a knife and cut into 1¼ in/3 cm pieces.

Pour the stock into a wok or pan; add the soya sauce, salt, peppercorns and coriander roots. Bring to a boil, then add the oxtail and boil for 10 minutes. Add the rest of the ingredients except the coriander leaves and boil until the potato is cooked, about 15 minutes. Remove from the heat and pour into bowls. Sprinkle with the coriander leaves.

Serve accompanied by rice.

SAI OOA

Northern Thai spicy sausages

• S E R V E S   S I X – E I G H T •
2 cups/12 oz/350 g minced (ground) fatty pork
½ spring onion, sliced finely
1 tbsp kaffir lime leaf, cut into fine strips
1 tbsp fish sauce
¼ tsp salt
20 in/½ metre sausage casing, rubbed with salt and rinsed
CHILLI PASTE
5 dried red chillies, chopped
1 tbsp chopped shallot
1 tbsp chopped garlic
½ tbsp chopped lemon grass
½ tsp chopped coriander root or stem
½ tsp chopped kaffir lime leaf
½ tsp shrimp paste
¼ tsp chopped galangal (ka)

Pound all the chilli paste ingredients to a fine paste with a mortar and pestle or in a blender. Mix the paste thoroughly in a bowl with the pork, spring onion (scallion), lime leaf, fish sauce and salt.

Stuff into the sausage casing. Tie the ends with string, coil into a spiral and prick with a toothpick. Roast in a 350°F/180°C/gas 4 oven until thoroughly cooked and nicely brown, about 15 minutes. Remove and cut into 1 in/2.5 cm slices.

Serve accompanied by lettuce, sliced shallots, small, hot chillies and sliced ginger.

LAAB DIP

Raw beef salad

Laab from the North of Thailand differs from the better-known Issaan version (see page 86), chiefly in that it does not include the roasted ground rice. Northerners also have a special liking for raw meat dishes. The origin for this and our more familiar steak tartare may well be the same: the chopped raw meat dish of the Mongols.

• S E R V E S   S I X •
7 oz/200 g very fresh lean beef sirloin, chopped finely at the last minute
2 oz/50 g beef liver, sliced thinly
½ cup/4 fl oz/100 ml very fresh beef blood
¼ cup/¼ oz/10 g mint leaves
3 tbsp finely sliced spring onion (scallion)
3 tbsp lime or lemon juice
½ tbsp fish sauce
1½ tsp chilli powder

Simply mix all the ingredients together well and place on serving plates.

Serve accompanied by raw morning glory (swamp cabbage), raw cabbage wedges, fresh basil and sticky rice.

NAM PHRIK ONG

Spicy meat and tomato dip

This is a relatively mild dip, and in Northern fashion, guests eat from the bowl in which it is served, scooping with the pork rind, vegetables or sticky rice.

• SERVES FOUR–SIX •
6 dried red chillies, chopped
3 tbsp chopped shallots
1 tbsp sliced lemon grass
1 tbsp chopped garlic
2 tsp shrimp paste
2 tsp salt
2 tbsp peanut or corn oil
½ cup/3 oz/75 g raw chopped pork
8 cherry tomatoes, diced
½ cup/4 fl oz/100 ml water
lemon juice, to taste
fish sauce, to taste
sugar, to taste
1 oz/25 g coriander leaves

Pound the chillies, onion, lemon grass, garlic, shrimp paste and salt together with a mortar and pestle or in a blender until fine.

Heat the oil in a wok or pan and add the chilli mixture and the pork and tomatoes. Cook until thick, about 15 minutes, then add the water and cook again for 10 minutes until thick.

Adjust the seasoning to taste with lemon juice, fish sauce and/or sugar. Garnish with the coriander leaves.

Serve accompanied by raw or slightly cooked vegetables, sticky rice, and if you can buy it, crispy pork rind (often sold under the Spanish name 'chicharrones').

NAM PHRIK NUM

Green chilli dip

High on the scale of chilli 'heat', but green and fresh-tasting. Intended to be eaten with sticky rice and assorted raw vegetables, and as part of a larger meal. Traditionally, everyone eats from one central bowl.

• SERVES SIX •
1 tbsp chopped dried salted mackerel or anchovy
4 tbsp peanut or corn oil
10 fresh 2 in/5 cm green chillies, chopped roughly
10 garlic cloves, chopped roughly
6 shallots, chopped roughly
3 cherry tomatoes
2 tbsp hot water
1 tbsp chopped spring onion (scallion)
1 tbsp chopped coriander leaves
fish sauce, to taste (optional)

Fry the dried fish in the oil over medium heat for about 7–10 minutes and drain. Dry-fry the chillies, garlic, shallots and tomatoes until fragrant, about 8–10 minutes. Place in a bowl. Pound them lightly with the dry fish. Add the water, spring onion (scallion) and coriander, and mix well. Taste to check: it should be of a saucy consistency and a touch salty; if not, add more water or fish sauce as required.

Serve accompanied by raw cabbage wedges, sliced cucumbers, raw green (string) beans and/or fried or roasted fish.

KHAO SOI

Curried noodles

A favourite lunch in Chiangmai and other Northern towns. The curry ingredients give away its Indian antecedents, but khao soi has arrived via Burma, in particular from the Shan States. Diners add the crispy noodles at the last minute so that they don't go soggy, and the condiments allow individual choice of flavour.

• SERVES FOUR–SIX •
6 cups/48 fl oz/1.35 ltr thin coconut milk
11 oz/300 g boneless skinned chicken breasts, cut lengthwise into ½ in/1 cm thick slices
1 tbsp white soya sauce
1 tbsp black soya sauce
2 tsp salt
15 oz/400 g dried or 7 oz/200 g fresh egg noodles (ba mii)
peanut or corn oil for frying
CHILLI PASTE
4 dried red chillies, chopped roughly
1 tbsp chopped shallot
2 tsp sliced ginger
1 tsp coriander seeds
1 tsp turmeric

Dry-roast the chilli paste ingredients in a 350°F/180°C/gas 4 oven until fragrant, about 8–10 minutes, then pound until fine with a mortar and pestle or in a blender.

Heat 1 cup/8 fl oz/225 ml of the coconut milk in a pan or wok, add the chilli paste and fry for 2 minutes, then add the chicken and soya sauces. Stir-fry for 3 minutes, then add the rest of the coconut milk and bring to a boil for 3 minutes. Add the salt and remove from the heat.

Fry 4 oz/100 g of the noodles in hot oil until crisp. Remove and drain well. Boil the rest of the noodles in water until firm but tender, about 6–8 minutes, and drain.

Place the boiled noodles in serving bowls, and pour the chicken mixture on top. Garnish with the fried noodles.

Serve accompanied by bowls of diced shallots, pickled cabbage and chilli powder.

KHANOM CHIIN NAM NGIO

White noodles with spicy meat sauce

This is the Northern version of khanom chiin, of which the standard recipe is described on page 24.

• SERVES FOUR–SIX •
¼ cup/2 fl oz/50 ml peanut or corn oil
11 oz/300 g minced (ground) pork
11 oz/300 g pork spare ribs, cut into 1 in/2.5 cm pieces
4 oz/100 g chicken blood pudding, cut into 1 in/2.5 cm pieces
6 cups/48 fl oz/1.35 ltr chicken stock
1 tbsp marinated black soya beans, pounded finely
1 tbsp salt
5 oz/150 g cherry tomatoes
15 oz/400 g fresh rice vermicelli (if dried, soak for 5 minutes and boil for 2 minutes) or cooked spaghetti
CHILLI PASTE
7 dried red chillies, chopped
1 oz/25 g garlic, chopped
½ oz/15 g shallot, chopped
2 tbsp chopped lemon grass
1 tbsp chopped galangal (ka)
1 tsp chopped coriander root or stem
1 tsp shrimp paste
1 tsp salt

Pound all the chilli paste ingredients together with a mortar and pestle or in a blender.

Heat the oil in a wok or pan, fry the chilli paste and then add the minced (ground) pork and spare ribs. Cook for 10 minutes, mixing well, then add the blood pudding, stock, soya beans and salt. Bring to a boil, add the tomatoes and simmer for 20 minutes or until the spare ribs are tender.

Boil the rice noodles in water until just done, 5–8 minutes, drain and place in serving bowls. Spoon the meat mixture over the noodles.

Serve accompanied by sliced fried garlic, deep-fried dried red chillies, spring onions (scallions), fresh coriander and lime wedges.

THE NORTH-EAST

The huge bulge of the country that borders the Mekong River in the North-east is culturally the most distinct of all the regions, with a culinary tradition that is much more Laotian than Thai. This is Issaan.

It is also Thailand's poorest region. In the cool, dry season from November onwards, the landscape is pleasant enough, although neither particularly beautiful nor interesting. It stretches, field after field, flat to the horizon; so flat that many villages are named after barely noticeable rises in the ground. Even more than the North, Issaan is the land of sticky rice; in the winter sunshine, villagers can be seen working in small groups, cutting rice to the swishing sound of their blades; in the small country towns and villages, pyramids of woven bamboo rice steamers stand for sale on the roadside.

A few months later, however, as the hot season brings to bite, the land bakes. The heat is a physical presence, and even the slow plod of a water buffalo kicks up low-hanging clouds of fine dust, slow to settle. Issaan poverty stems from its infamous droughts. Even when the rains come on time, they are often insufficient, and in some years they simply fail. Under the eaves of virtually every house stands one or more giant earthenware water jars, some five feet (one and a half metres) tall, and as wide, to catch the run-off from any rain that falls.

One of the effects of the Northeastern droughts is the migration of workers to the capital, Bangkok. Not all go permanently; many stay just for the months between planting and harvest, to earn city wages that they can take home. Inevitably, Issaan food has followed, and a common sight in Bangkok lanes and on street-corners is vendors selling *som tam thai,* the green papaya salad. In the last few years Issaan restaurants have enjoyed a minor boom in the capital, and although the country fieriness of this distinctive cuisine is as strange to the palates of most Bangkok Thais as it is to Westerners, it has caught on. One of my favourites is a restaurant called Issaan Classic, on Ploenchit Road near the British Embassy . . . although its owners have clearly taken an independent approach to English translation by hanging an illuminated sign outside announcing its name as 'Isn't Classic'!

RIGHT: *An old woman sells spices in a street market.*

BELOW: *Part of the Elephant Festival. Elephants are still an important part of life in some parts of Thailand.*

LEFT *Buffaloes have a reputation for being fierce, but in fact are usually very gentle with those who look after them. This child is taking the animals home at the end of the day.*

LAAB KAI

Spiced minced (ground) chicken

One of the special characteristics of the North-eastern version of this chopped meat dish is the addition of uncooked sticky rice that is first roasted (either in an oven or in a dry wok) until golden and then pounded in a mortar. It adds a slightly nutty flavour and gives the dish more body.

• SERVES SIX •
1 lb/450 g finely minced (ground) chicken
¼ cup/1½ oz/40 g sliced shallots
¼ cup/¼ oz/10 g coriander leaves
4 tbsp sticky rice, dry-fried for 8–10 minutes until brown and pounded finely
4 tbsp lemon juice, or to taste
3 tbsp fish sauce, or to taste
1 tbsp chopped dried red chilli, or to taste
½ tsp sugar
fresh mint leaves for garnish

Cook the chicken in a non-stick pan over low heat for 10 minutes – do not add water or oil. When cooked, transfer to a bowl and mix in well all the remaining ingredients except the mint. Check the seasoning, and add more lemon juice, fish sauce or chilli if necessary. Sprinkle the mint over the top to garnish.

Serve accompanied by raw cabbage leaves, spring onions (scallions) and raw green (string) beans.

KAI YANG

Grilled (broiled) chicken

The Issaan version of a dish that appears in many cuisines. Here, the marinade makes a distinctive difference.

• SERVES FOUR •
3 lb/1.35 kg whole chicken, split in half
10 garlic cloves, chopped finely
2 tbsp black peppercorns, crushed
2 tbsp white soya sauce
2 tbsp sugar
2 tbsp brandy or sherry
1 tsp salt
SAUCE
1 cup/8 fl oz/225 ml white vinegar
½ cup/3 oz/75 g sugar
3 garlic cloves, fresh or marinated, chopped roughly
2 fresh red chillies, pounded well
½ tbsp salt

Mix the chicken with all the ingredients (apart from the sauce) in a bowl and leave to marinate for 3–4 hours. Grill (broil) over charcoal for 30 minutes, turning occasionally, or roast in a 350°F/180°C/gas 4 oven for 40 minutes, turning half-way through.

Meanwhile, mix all the sauce ingredients together and boil in a pan over medium heat until thick. Cool and serve with the roasted chicken.

Serve accompanied by sticky or steamed rice and som tam thai (see page 93).

NEUA YANG

Grilled (broiled) beef

A good dish for summer barbecues.

• SERVES FOUR–SIX •
1 lb 2 oz/500 g beef with some fat on it (sirloin)
3 tsp white soya sauce

Rub the steak with the soya sauce and leave in the refrigerator for 3 hours. Grill (broil) under high heat for 10–15 minutes, turning once, or roast in a 350°F/180°C/gas 4 oven until done to your preference. Slice thinly.

Serve accompanied by sticky rice, sliced cucumber and nam chim sauce (see lin yang, page 88).

LIN YANG

Grilled (broiled) tongue

• SERVES FOUR •
1 lb 2 oz/500 g whole beef tongue
1 tsp salt
1 tsp black soya sauce
½ tsp sugar
¼ tsp white soya sauce
2 tbsp peanut or corn oil
NAM CHIM
2 tbsp fish sauce
1 dried red chilli, pounded
1 tbsp sticky rice, dry-fried for a few minutes and
pounded finely
½ tbsp lemon juice
½ tbsp chopped spring onion (scallion)
1 tsp sliced shallot
⅛ tsp sugar

Clean the tongue and rub it with the salt, black soya sauce, sugar and white soya sauce. Chill in the refrigerator for 1 hour, then rub with the oil and grill (broil) under medium heat or roast, uncovered, in a 350°F/180°C/gas 4 oven for 15–20 minutes or until the juices run clear when pierced with a fork. Turn over after 10 minutes.

Remove and slice across into thin oval pieces. Mix the ingredients for the nam chim sauce together and serve with the tongue.

Serve accompanied by rice.

NAM TOK

Sliced beef salad

• SERVES FOUR–SIX •
11 oz/300 g beef sirloin
½ tsp salt
½ tsp ground white pepper
½ tbsp fish sauce, or to taste
½ cup/4 fl oz/100 ml pork or chicken stock
3 spring onions (scallions), sliced finely
¼ cup/1 oz/25 g sliced shallots
15 mint leaves
2 tbsp sticky rice, dry-fried for a few minutes and
pounded finely
2 tbsp lime or lemon juice, or to taste
1 tbsp pounded dried red chilli, or to taste
1 tsp sugar

Season the beef with salt, pepper and the ½ tbsp of fish sauce. Grill (broil) under a high heat until done to your liking, about 7 minutes on each side. Slice thinly.

Mix all the remaining ingredients well in a bowl and stir in the beef slices. Check the seasoning, adding more fish sauce, chilli or lemon juice to taste.

Serve accompanied by raw cabbage wedges, fresh basil, lettuce and any other raw vegetables, and rice.

TAP WAAN

Spicy liver salad

A little spicy, but a very good and unusual way to serve liver.

• S E R V E S   F O U R •
¼ cup/2 fl oz/50 ml chicken stock
11 oz/300 g beef liver, sliced thinly
¼ cup/1 oz/25 g sliced shallots
¼ cup/1¼ oz/10 g mint leaves
3 spring onions (scallions), chopped finely
¼ cup/2 fl oz/50 ml lime or lemon juice
2 tbsp sticky rice, dry-fried for a few minutes and pounded finely
2 tbsp crushed dried red chilli
2 tbsp fish sauce

Bring the chicken stock in a pan to a boil, add the liver and cook until medium-rare. Remove the pan from the heat, drain and stir in the rest of the ingredients. Mix well and transfer to a serving plate.

Serve accompanied by raw green (string) beans, morning glory (swamp cabbage), cabbage leaves, fresh basil and sticky rice.

LAP PLAA DUK

Spicy catfish salad

• S E R V E S   F O U R •
11 oz/300 g whole catfish, cleaned and gutted
1 tbsp peanut or corn oil
¼ cup/¼ oz/10 g mint leaves, sliced
3 tbsp lime juice, or to taste
3 tbsp sliced shallots
2½ tbsp fish sauce, or to taste
1½ tbsp sticky rice, dry-fried for a few minutes and pounded finely
1 tsp chilli powder
1 tsp finely shredded kaffir lime leaf

Rub the catfish with the oil and roast in the oven at 350°F/180°C/gas 4 oven for 40 minutes until firm but tender. When cooked, remove the skin and bones and chop the fish meat finely. Place in a bowl and stir in the rest of the ingredients – mix well. Check the seasoning, and add more fish sauce or lime juice if you like.

Serve accompanied by raw green (string) beans, cabbage, sweet basil and spring onions (scallions).

TOM SAEP

Issaan-style soup

• SERVES FOUR–SIX •

4 oz/100 g each of beef or calf's heart, liver, lung, kidney and small intestines (any offal may be used, depending on your preference), cleaned and prepared
5 cups/40 fl oz/1.25 ltr water
1 oz/25 g galangal (ka), sliced
3 stalks of lemon grass, cut into 1¼ in/3 cm pieces and crushed
5 kaffir lime leaves, shredded
1½ tbsp fish sauce
1 tbsp lemon juice
2 dried red chillies, crushed
½ tsp salt
1 spring onion (scallion), cut into ½ in/1 cm pieces

Boil all the offal together in a pan of water until tender, about 30–40 minutes. Rinse well in cold water and slice all up fairly small.

Place the cooked offal in a pan with the water, bring to a boil and add all the remaining ingredients except the spring onion (scallion). Bring back to boil for 2 minutes, add the spring onion (scallion) and remove from the heat. Serve immediately.

Serve accompanied by sticky or steamed rice.

KAENG NORMAI

Bamboo shoot soup

• S E R V E S   F O U R – S I X •

2½ cups/20 fl oz/550 ml water
3 tbsp chopped dried salted mackerel or anchovies
1 stalk of lemon grass, cut into ¾ in/2 cm pieces and crushed lightly
3 kaffir lime leaves, torn into small pieces
2½ oz/60 g pumpkin flesh, cut into ¾ in/2 cm pieces
2½ oz/60 g bamboo shoots, sliced
1 oz/25 g green (string) beans, cut into ¾ in/2 cm pieces
3 small white aubergines (eggplants), quartered
3 fresh small green chillies, crushed lightly
3 fresh large green chillies, cut into thirds
1 tbsp fish sauce
½ cup/½ oz/15 g lemon basil leaves

Boil the water in a pan or wok and add the dried fish, lemon grass and lime leaf. Boil for 1 minute, add the rest of the ingredients except the lemon basil and simmer for 7–10 minutes or until the pumpkin is soft. Stir in the basil and remove from the heat immediately.

Serve accompanied by rice.

SUP NORMAI

Shredded bamboo shoot

Although called a soup, there is no stock, and this dish is really more like a salad.

• S E R V E S   S I X •

2 cups/1 lb 2 oz/500 g bamboo shoots, cut into long matchsticks
2 spring onions (scallions), sliced
10 mint leaves
2 tbsp sticky rice, dry-fried for a few minutes and pounded
2 tbsp lemon juice
2 tbsp sliced red onion
½ tbsp fish sauce
1 dried red chilli, pounded

Boil the bamboo shoots in water until tender but not soft, about 10 minutes if fresh, or 1 minute if canned. Strain (discard the water) and rinse shoots well in cold water. Put in a bowl and mix well with all the remaining ingredients.

Serve accompanied by roasted chicken and raw vegetables.

KAENG PAA MOO PAA

Wild boar country curry

Well, wild boar is not strictly necessary (and in any case in Thailand these days is bred, not hunted). Substitute pork.

• SERVES FOUR •
¼ cup/2 fl oz/50 ml peanut or corn oil
8 oz/225 g boar or pork loin, cut into 1¼ × ¾ × ¼ in/
3 × 2 × 1 cm slices
5 cups/40 fl oz/1.25 ltr water
7 oz/200 g bamboo shoots, diced
5 oz/150 g small white aubergines (eggplants)
4½ oz/120 g green (string) beans
¼ cup/1½ oz/40 g krachai, sliced lengthwise
3 fresh red chillies, quartered lengthwise
2 tbsp fish sauce
3 kaffir lime leaves, torn into small pieces
¼ cup/¼ oz/10 g sweet basil leaves
CHILLI PASTE
1 oz/25 g shallots, chopped
1 oz/25 g garlic cloves, chopped
½ oz/15 g dried red chillies, chopped
2 coriander roots, chopped
1 tbsp chopped lemon grass
1 tsp chopped galangal (ka)
1 tsp chopped kaffir lime zest
1 tsp salt
½ tsp shrimp paste

Pound all the chilli paste ingredients together with a mortar and pestle or in a blender to a fine paste.

Heat the oil in a wok or pan and fry the chilli paste for 3 minutes. Add the meat and stir-fry for 2 minutes; then add the water and bamboo shoots and cook until the shoots are tender, about 3–5 minutes. Add the aubergines (eggplants), green (string) beans, krachai, chillies, fish sauce and lime leaf, boil for 3 minutes more and then remove from the heat. Stir in the basil and serve.

Serve accompanied by pickled garlic, salted eggs and sticky rice.

SAI KROK ISSAAN

North-eastern sausages

• SERVES FOUR–SIX •

1 cup/6 oz/175 g minced (ground) pork
¼ cup/1½ oz/40 g cooked rice
2 tbsp lime juice
1 tsp chopped garlic
1 tsp ground white pepper
½ tsp salt
¼ tsp sugar
20 in/½ metre sausage casing, rubbed with salt and rinsed
approx. 2 cups/16 fl oz/450 ml peanut or corn oil for frying

Take the pork, rice, lime juice, garlic, pepper, salt and sugar, and mix well. Stuff into the sausage casing, and tie along the length with string into small balls. Chill in the refrigerator for 24 hours.

Prick the sausage with a toothpick. Heat the oil to 350°F/ 180°C in a pan and fry the sausage on both sides until brown and well cooked, about 15 minutes. Cut into individual sausages.

Serve accompanied by fresh sliced ginger, fresh cabbage, fresh cabbage, fresh small green chillies, peanuts, spring onions (scallions) and coriander leaves.

SOM TAM THAI

Green papaya salad

Although unripe papaya is not easy to buy in the West, this famous North-eastern dish is well worth the trouble. Som tam stalls are a common sight throughout not only the North-east but also all major cities and towns. Much of the popularity of this dish, traditionally eaten with sticky rice, is its combination of sweet and sour flavours.

• SERVES FOUR •

11 oz/300 g green papaya, peeled and cut into long matchsticks
7 fresh small whole green chillies
6 garlic cloves, chopped roughly
½ cup/2 oz/50 g green (string) beans cut into 1 in/2.5 cm pieces
¼ cup/2½ oz/60 g unsalted roasted peanuts
¼ cup/1 oz/25 g dried small shrimps
6 cherry tomatoes, quartered
¼ cup/2 fl oz/50 ml lime or lemon juice
1 tbsp palm sugar
1 tbsp fish sauce

Take a little of the papaya, the chilli and garlic, and pound together lightly with a mortar and pestle or in a blender. Put in a bowl and stir in the beans, peanuts, shrimp, tomato and the rest of the papaya. Mix well, then stir in the lemon juice, sugar and fish sauce.

Serve accompanied by raw vegetables chopped into bite-sized pieces – perhaps morning glory (swamp cabbage) and green (string) beans – sticky rice and roasted chicken.

JEOW BONG

North-eastern spicy dip

This dip is not very spicy, but has an interesting combination of flavours.

• SERVES FOUR–SIX •
6 garlic cloves
1 tbsp sliced shallot
1 tsp chopped galangal (ka)
2 tbsp finely chopped anchovies
1 tbsp lemon juice
1 dried red chilli, pounded finely
1 kaffir lime leaf, torn into small pieces
½ stalk of lemon grass, sliced finely

Dry-fry the garlic, shallot and galangal for 3 minutes over medium heat, then chop finely. Pound with the rest of the ingredients with a mortar and pestle or in a blender.

Serve accompanied by cabbage, green (string) beans, fresh basil and sticky rice.

PLAA RAA SAWNG KREUNG

Fermented dip for vegetables and rice

North-easterners have their own special version of fish sauce, a much more substantial affair containing fish pieces, vegetables and flavourings. Quite pungent!

• SERVES SIX–EIGHT •
2½ cups/20 fl oz/550 ml thin coconut milk
3 oz/75 g dried salted mackerel (the smellier the better) or anchovies
1½ oz/40 g galangal (ka), sliced
1½ oz/40 g lemon grass, sliced
5 oz/150 g catfish fillets, skinned and cut into pieces
6 fresh small whole red chillies
1 tbsp finely sliced kaffir lime leaves
1½ oz/40 g krachai, cut into lengthwise matchsticks
4 oz/100 g green (string) beans, cut into 1 in/2.5 cm pieces
2 oz/50 g shallots, halved
2 oz/50 g bamboo shoots, cut into ¼ in/5 mm cubes
4 baby white aubergines (eggplants), the size of large grapes
fish sauce, to taste (optional)

Heat the coconut milk in a pan, add the salted fish, boil for 1 minute, add the galangal and lemon grass, boil again, then add the catfish, chillies and lime leaf and cook for another minute. Add the krachai – don't stir it in – and bring back to a boil. Simmer for 3 minutes, add the rest of the ingredients and cook for another 2 minutes. Taste for saltiness and add fish sauce as necessary. Serve hot or cold – this dish can be refrigerated for 2–3 days to enhance the flavours.

Serve accompanied by raw vegetables and rice.

INDEX

met kanoon 30–1
mieng kum 76
moo krathiam phrik thai 52
moo satei 72–3
Muslim curry 69
mussel
  pancakes, fried 38
  and pineapple curry soup 20
  salad, spicy 37

N

nam phrik jon 71
nam phrik num 81
nam phrik ong 81
nam phrik pla too 26
nam tok 88
neua yang 87
noodles
  curried83
  fried with chicken, vegetables and gravy 45
  glass, casseroled prawns with 55
  soup 56
  sweet crisp-fried 56–7
  Thai-fried 23
  white, with sauce 24, 83

O

omelette, stuffed 64
oxtail soup 79

P

panaeng neua 68
pancakes, fried mussel 38
papaya salad 92
pepper, green, chicken fried with 48
phad sator 72
phak bung fai daeng 62
phak phad ruam mit 63
phrik nam plaa 25
pineapple and mussel curry soup 20
pineapple rice 59
plaa jian 53
plaa nung manao phrik sod 35
plaa phao 34
plaa raa sawng kreung 94
plaa raad phrik 34
po taek 36
poo jaa 39
poo phao pong karil 39
popia sod 61
pork
  curry 78, 92
  fried flat beans with 72
  fried with garlic and peppercorns 52
  and ginger with fried fish 53
  red, with rice 52
  satei 72–3
  and spinach curry soup 77
pork and coconut sauce 24
prawns/shrimp
  casserold with glass noddles 55
  with coconut milk and chilli paste 36
  fried with garlic and pepper 35

  with lemon and coconut 53
  shrimp-fried rice 35
  soup, hot and sour 22
  spicy vegetable soup 79
priaw waan kai 46
pumpkin, coconut custard in 27

R

red chicken curry 19
red duck curry 50–1
red pork with rice 52
rice
  chicken 43, 44
  crackers with pork and coconut sauce 24
  duck with 50
  fermented dip for 94
  fried, with spicy sauce 58
  pineapple 59
  red pork with 52
  salad 71
  shrimp-fried 35
  soup, boiled, with chicken 57
  sticky, with mangoes 29
roti 73

S

sai krok issaan 92
sai ooa 80
salad
  green mango 25
  green papaya 92
  raw beef 80
  rice 71
  roasted aubergine 60
  sliced beef 88
  spicy catfish 53, 89
  spicy liver 89
  spicy mussel 37
  spicy seafood salad 37
sangkhyaa fak thong 27
satei, pork 72–3
sauce
  fish with chillies 25
  pork and coconut 24
  spicy, fried rice with 58
  spicy meat, with white noodles 83
sausages
  north-eastern 92
  spicy 80
seafood
  salad, spicy 37
  see also shellfish
seafood soup 36
shellfish see clams; crab; mussels; prawns/shrimp
shrimp see prawns/shrimp
smoked fish soup 22
som tam thai 92
soup
  bamboo shoot 91
  boiled rice, with chicken 57
  coconut and galangal 21
  hot and sour prawn 22
  Issaan-style 90
  mussel and pineapple curry 20
  noodle 56

northern Thai 79
oxtail 79
seafood 36
smoked fish 22
sour curry 70
spicy vegetable with prawns/shrimp 79
spinach curry and pork 77
stuffed squid 21
sour curry soup 70
southern vegetable dip 71
spicy catfish salad 53, 89
spicy dip 94
spicy dip with mackerel 26
spicy fried frogs' legs 25
spicy liver salad 89
spicy meat sauce, white noodles with 83
spicy meat and tomato dip 81
spicy mussel salad 37
spicy sausages 80
spicy seafood salad 37
spicy vegetable soup with prawns/shrimp 79
spinach, curry soup and pork 77
spring rolls, fresh 61
squid soup, stuffed 21
steamed fish curry 20
stuffed crab shells 39
stuffed omelette 64
stuffed squid soup 21
sup normai 91
sweet crisp-fried noodles 56–7
sweet and sour chicken 46

T

tap waan 89
Thai-fried noodles 23
thong yod 30
tom hang wua 79
tom khaa kai 21
tom klong plaa krob 22
tom saep 90
tom yum kung 22
tomato, and spicy meat dip 81
tongue, grilled (broiled) 88

V

vegetables
  dip 71, 94
  soup, spicy, with prawns/shrimp 79
  stir-fried 62, 63
  see also beans

W

white noodles with sauce 24

Y

yam hoi malaeng poo 37
yam ma muang 25
yam makheua yao 60
yam plaa duk foo 53
yam thalae 37
yellow chicken curry 68